Warrior Culture

Published by Bad Dog Press
302 Northgate Mall Drive, Suite 1413
Hixson, TN 37343-9998

Cover art by Micah Hughes
Book design by Josh Templeton
Edited by Abbie Templeton and Cole Rose

ISBN: 978-0-9980624-4-0

To all the people I've had the privilege to coach,
Especially the 2018-2020 Boyd Buchanan Bucs led
by Cam Baubach, Riley Covington,
Preston Edmondson, Will Emrey,
Eli Evans, Trent Gilley,
Ian Johnson, and Jacob Oliver,
Thank you for the inspiration.

TABLE OF CONTENTS

Warrior Culture

The Warrior Way for High School Teams

Josh Templeton

Warrior Culture Wins

Throughout history, People have grappled with fear. The fear that comes with competition, taking risks, and losing what we have. Time after time, great Warrior Cultures have recognized the necessity to confront fear in order to conquer it. The courage to unflinchingly face fear and strive to overcome it is a staple of success in all cultures. But none have articulated this fact as well as Warrior Cultures. Knowing that the end is inevitable, the true Warrior puts a premium on the battle, the process, doing the right thing in the moment, instead of the victory itself. Tackling fear head-on liberates the Warrior from its paralyzing effects and empowers them to fight at their highest level. This truth serves as a powerful metaphor in our daily lives. This is why regular people from all walks of life are inspired by the Warrior Way.

Our players often fight an internal battle with fear. Performance anxiety. Not being good enough. Fear of losing. And many more. Fear can have an adverse effect on an athlete's ability to compete at a high level. A question we, as coaches, should be asking is how can we help our athletes confront and conquer their fear.

We've all heard people say, "You can't teach toughness. They either are, or they ain't." There have been times in my coaching career, I believed that to be true. Not anymore.

I've also heard, "Kids these days just aren't tough anymore." I once thought that, too. But now I think it might be a self-righteous load of crap. And lazy coaching.

I'm not a coaching theory expert telling you how to run your program with catchy soundbites and minimal shared experience. I'm just a high school basketball coach trying to make a difference in the lives of young people. Just like you. I've taught in the classrooms, walked the sidelines, called the timeouts, and sat in difficult parent meetings.

To be perfectly clear from the jump, this book is NOT about militarizing high school sports. And any reader expecting advocation for authoritarian coaching philosophy will be greatly disappointed. This book will focus on understanding, connecting with, and inspiring players to be better, stronger people. And we must be intentional about developing purity in the hearts of athletes so they can become valuable members of teams.

I'll share ideas that have worked for our programs, mistakes I've made, lessons learned from my experiences as a competitor and a coach, and wisdom shared by my friends and mentors.

Coaching high school sports is a challenging and demanding job. But it can also be so rewarding. We get the opportunity to overcome obstacles with our creative ingenuity. We get to be a positive influence on a younger generation who watches us, asks us how, tries to please us, and desperately wants to be proud of themselves. And we have learned that our character will carry more weight with our players than our instructions. For these reasons, coaching helps us to grow ourselves.

Bad days find us all, and if 2020 taught us anything, it's that life often punches down. Fear is real. Pain is real. And they are not to be avoided, but confronted head on so we can live well. Do better. Be better. Respect ourselves.
Why? Because we want to be Warriors.

The way to our best lives is unleashing the Warrior Spirit within us. And I have found that the most successful, inspiring people to walk this planet tapped into this spirit.

We'll coach a plethora of unique personalities during our careers. But for simplicity's sake, we'll discuss three types of competitive mindsets in this book, Civilians, Nameless, and Warriors.

Civilians are just there. The general population. They live in a way that doesn't require them to walk the hard path. They just are.

Some have poisoned their own mind with their self-talk. At their worst, they have a hard time getting over themselves. Their lives exist in a bubble of comfort. Everything is about them. And they can't wait to tell us all about it. Who wronged them. Why things are inconvenient for them. What people should do for them.

They don't feel responsible to solve their problems, but they complain a lot. They're easy to spot. They lack empathy. Their social media posts often reveal character deficiencies they refuse to accept. Entitlement is prevalent. They are toxic liabilities to their school, workplace, or worse, society as a whole. Most of these people can't be helped until they hit bottom and realize that the problem is them. Until that happens, any coaching is a waste of breath.

But many civilians are just doing the best they can with what they know. They would like to be a Warrior. But the thing is, they just don't know how. They aren't sure what the Warrior path looks like. Or how it applies to them where they are.

Their potential is like a box of fireworks waiting for someone to ignite the fuse so they can light up the sky, bringing smiles to the faces of strangers. They are standing in front of a blank canvas, desperate to paint their masterpiece. They just need an artist to show them how to master the craft. A mentor. Most high school athletes are like these civilians when they first step onto our practice floor. As coaches, we are mentors who can foster personal growth and development. Many of us chose this profession for that reason.

Now here they are, and it's our job to teach them how to paint their masterpiece. And if we truly are the Warriors, generals, teachers, coaches that we claim to be, we will show them the Warrior Path they didn't even know they wanted to take. We won't complain about who they are not. We'll love and accept the person they are and believe in the Warrior they're becoming.

Nameless fight, but their performance in battle is limited by either their limited abilities or their minds. They are valuable to teams. But they may not stand out. They fight and are often respected. If a nameless is limited by their abilities in one activity but overcomes the self-imposed limitations of their minds, they can become Warriors in an area of performance that is more suited to their skill set later in life. The pure-hearted nameless may not be Warriors yet, but they can gain the mental tools to become.

Warriors fight and become legends. They relentlessly pursue excellence, overcome mental barriers, and accomplish things that amaze. They embrace the hardships of life and welcome the challenge. They crave competition because they live to unleash the fighting spirit inside them. They fight to win every time, but get as much enjoyment out of a great fight as they do a big win. They don't work for accolades. They work to become the best they can be at something they love to do. They let their emotions enhance their abilities, but never hinder them.

They are honest and self-aware. They understand the value of a positive outlook and the need for critical analysis. They are resilient. They don't complain about problems, they solve them. They grow more confident every day. They live by a code of ethics and make decisions for moral reasons, not emotional ones.

They want how they compete and live their lives to be remembered. And when a Warrior inevitably falls short of who they want to be, they own it, learn from it, and get back on their horse, sword in hand, and activate, moving on to their next best action. A Warrior is respected. A Warrior inspires.

So here we go, stories of the Warrior Spirit in history and sports that inspire. Quotes that will encourage us to stay on the path. And how we can apply Warrior philosophy to our teams. The big winners here will be our players who became Warriors on a court or field. And when they carry the Warrior Spirit into adulthood, they'll be ready for any obstacle life can throw at them.

Warrior Culture Wins.

PART 1:
The Warrior Coach

BUCS: OVERCOMING A LOSING CULTURE

Being familiar with the Bucs tradition of excellence and the pride that the community had in their athletic programs, I was excited about my new coaching opportunity at Boyd Buchanan School in 2018. But after watching the football games in the fall before we began our first season together, excitement wasn't the word. There weren't words that could accurately express the level of my concern. But there was a thought—*What have I gotten myself into?*

Our football team—who consisted of many basketball players—went 0-10. But it wasn't the bagel on the front of the record that bothered me. It was the way they didn't compete. They laid down for their opponents every game. Absolutely no fight in this dog. There is a mercy rule in Tennessee high school football—the clock runs in the second half if a team leads by 35 points or more. The clock never stopped in a second half in any of our games that season. Going into each game, our Bucs knew their fate, so they didn't even try.

I knew coming into basketball season that this year wouldn't be about basketball. Our athletes needed to address the heart before they could even think about winning basketball games.

So... "You can't teach toughness."
Well, our staff didn't have a choice. We had to try. I didn't realize it at the time, but I had learned so many things over the course of my playing, coaching, and even professional career outside of basketball that

prepared me for this team. It felt like my entire journey had brought me to this place. A place with the best chance to attempt to do the best thing coaches can do—impact the hearts and minds of our players.

Now, I realize there are certain expectations when reading a book about coaching. You're probably expecting a lot of theory and a fail-safe plan. Here's the thing—that fail-safe plan doesn't exist, and theory often gets exploited by variables. It's these variables we love most about sports and the stories within the games. Besides the obvious (A zero-sports quarantine), why did we glue ourselves to the TV to watch *The Last Dance* on ESPN in the spring of 2020? Why do we watch any story unfold, fiction or reality, with unflinching attention?

It's the variables. Drama, parody, obstacles to overcome, etc. If it weren't for the variables, life would be a soulless grind, and sports would be boring. The only people who want sports to be predictable are bettors and handicappers. The rest of us want a show. We want to feel the exhilaration of an underdog victory. We want our hearts broken in soul crushing defeat. We want to see athletes get knocked to the canvas, and against all odds, rise to their feet and attempt the unbelievable. And most of all, we want to be inspired.

So that's where we start. My team of puppies who weren't sure if they had it in them to be dogs. We had to paint an enticing picture of the beasts they could be. We had to show them what that athlete looked like in action. We had to model how that person acted every day. And they had to answer one question to be on our team—do I want to be a Warrior?

Deep down, I believe that most people have a common desire—to be respected. People can be respected simply because of what they do. But the Warrior craves respect that inspires those around them. It's not what they do, it's the way they do it. But there's a big difference between wanting to be a Warrior and having the knowledge, ability, discipline, and courage to make it happen. And even more, to become a Warrior whose passion inspires people.

The Warrior lives by a certain code. Many call it the path. One thing is clear, there is something in the Warrior that isn't in everyone else.

We don't have to fight in wars or enter a ring to walk the path, but we have to adopt a code. A way of life. If studying Warrior Culture has taught us anything, it is the code can be applied to every aspect of life. The Warrior knows that in the end, no matter what happens, there will be ultimate respect of self. And what better gift could we give our athletes than inspiring them to pursue self-respect.

I won't coach people I don't respect anymore. It's a waste of time and energy. And I've found it nearly impossible to respect someone who doesn't respect themselves. The Warrior Path may not be for everyone, and that's fine. There's an activity out there for them. Preferably, one that isn't competitive.

From what I've seen these last few years with our Bucs, kids haven't changed that much. And they're capable of so much more than we often think they are. I truly believe that most athletes want to be tough, respected, and viewed as a Warrior.

Maybe it's on us. Maybe we stopped showing them how. Maybe we stopped modeling the Warrior way in our own lives. It's possible that "kids just aren't tough as they used to be" actually means—we, as adults, don't put a premium on showing them how to become Warriors. We only tell them how they fall short. There has to be a better way.

Appeal to the *person* they want to be, not just the *player* we want them to be. Inspire them to become someone they can respect. Hold them accountable to the code they've adopted. And in all things, celebrate the heck out of every step they take on the Warrior Path. If we show them what a Warrior looks like, before we know it, we'll be coaching a team of them and loving every second.

The Warrior's career will end, but the heart of the Warrior never dies. They will leave sports behind and go on to greatness in their adult lives. Living their code to become the husbands and wives, dads and moms, entrepreneurs, business executives, teachers, coaches, doctors, writers, and team members. Basically... the human being they've always wanted to be. One who makes a difference in the world around them. The Warrior who inspires.

Aside from parents, a coach has arguably the most influential voice in the life of a serious athlete. Let's shoulder the responsibility and inspire our players to become the Warrior. This book is about showing them how.

Chapter 1

The General

General George Patton is one of the most celebrated military leaders in U.S. history. History shows that he was a flawed man with a big ego, occasionally letting emotion undermine his decision-making. The same could be said of most men, whether leading or following. But the consensus remains that, at his best, his men loved him, and he was a strategic genius.

In World War 2, his inspired third army played a key role in the Allied victory. One thing is sure, Patton could motivate his men.

June 1944, Patton gave a speech to his men. A less profane, abbreviated version of this speech was portrayed in the 1970 film, *Patton,*[1] placing him in the stratosphere of Warrior culture history. To this day, hairs on the arms of U.S. soldiers stand up straight when they hear it. Their hearts beat faster. With every

---

[1] *Patton.* Directed by Franklin J. Shaffner, screenplay by Francis Ford Coppola and Edmund H. North, performance by George C. Scott, 20th Century-Fox, 1970.

passing sentence, the desire to run through a brick wall grows in the hearts of fighting men.

Patton could relate to the Warrior because he was one to his core. He modeled the Warrior way with his actions and earned the respect of his men. Men who have fought for him recount Patton fetching gas cans for the vehicles and making sure they always had a hot meal during breaks from battle. He took care of them. He served. For this reason, they loved him. And because they loved him, his words held lasting impact. It's important to remember that our words will not hold the weight we desire if we don't live up to them.

As coaches, we must embrace the fact that our words are one of our greatest weapons. We won't take a shot or kick a field goal, but if we can channel our Warrior Spirit and combine it with empathy for our players, we can serve our teams by articulating the things they may not even realize they are feeling. We can get to their hearts, empowering them to stay on the path of the Warrior they want to become.

Have you ever felt something in your soul that you couldn't put into words? Then you read an article or book, or listened to a podcast, or watched a video that perfectly articulated this truth you've always known. And you were like... *YES!*

We've all experienced that. And we perform better as a result, not because we learned something new, but because we have a deeper understanding of ourselves and the people we want to be. The information and the way it's presented serves as a reminder. Speaking is an important aspect of coaching. And if we desire to maximize our effectiveness, we should be articulate, empathetic, and... wait for it... entertaining.

Why do motivational videos on YouTube get millions of views? Is it because people are hungry for knowledge? I'd argue that people are hungry to be kicked reminded of the greatness that exists within them. And that's exactly what the best influencers in the world do.

Coaches love some good analytical breakdowns, so here's a little breakdown of the highlights of one of the greatest military speeches in American history.

THE POWER OF LANGUAGE

"Men, this stuff that some sources sling around about America wanting out of this war, not wanting to fight, is a crock of bullshit."
—General George Patton, US Army, June 5, 1944

Strong language loosens people up, especially articulate profanity peppered with humor. In the book *The Unknown Patton* by Charles M. Province, Patton was quoted, "When I want my men to remember something, to really make it stick, I give it to them double dirty. It may not sound nice to some bunch of little old ladies at an afternoon tea party, but it helps my soldiers to remember. You can't run an army without profanity: and it has to be eloquent profanity. An army without profanity couldn't fight its way out of a piss-soaked paper bag... As for the type of comments I make, sometimes I just, By God, get carried away with my own eloquence."[2]

To be clear, this is not advocation for the use of profanity as a high school coach. In many school environments, especially in Christian schools, profanity is forbidden. And as coaches representing a school's core values, our actions and our words must be in line with those values. This is true even if these values don't line up with our personal values. If that's an issue, the job shouldn't have been accepted in the first place.

Our environment should affect the language we use. We can say the right thing in the wrong setting and be wrong. We can say the right thing at the wrong time and be wrong. If speaking to an audience of 4th grade boys at a private school about toughness, it wouldn't be a great idea to drop vulgarity bombs on the mic, especially if they're taking notes.

If speaking to US Marines about the same thing, the same language used with the 4th graders isn't recommended. The points on the subject may be similar, but the appropriate language will be vastly different. The difference in those audience examples are extreme, but teams of high school athletes will land somewhere in the middle. Knowing our environment and audience is key.

---

[2] Province, Charles M. *The Unknown Patton.* Random House Value Publishing, 1988

Every situation is different, and if a little profanity is acceptable where we work, we need to treat it with care and be really good at it. Because profanity, like many other things in life, can have polarized emotional effects. It's best used with calm objectivity. It's worst used with impromptu emotionalism.

For example, profanity directed at a player[3] could feel like a direct attack, and through the lens of some players, it is abusive language. This should never be done, even in jest.

The reality of profanity in jest is most people correlate profanity, regardless of their moral position on it, with unfiltered honesty. This is why influencers like Tony Robbins and Gary Vaynerchuk are so effective. Their language is powerful because they are honest and it's who they are. Others could use the same language and sound inauthentic because it doesn't fit their personality at all. It comes out awkwardly. And there's disconnect with the audience because people can sense even subtle dishonesty.

We don't have to cuss. It just takes a little more effort to master effective motivational speech. If cursing is against a school's or coach's personal values, the coach will need to be articulate and creative with their language to maximize the power of speech in their competitive, intense environment.

---

[3] "You are a [insert curse]"

My dad never cursed to his team, but he is a master story teller. Dick Devenzio, the late author and founder of Point Guard College (PGC), used acronyms to make ideas sticky. And PGC still uses this tactic effectively today, maximizing the stickiness of the concepts they teach. Like this...

Calm
Unthreatening
Restraint
Sincere
Environment

So, if it's true to your personality, proceed with precision and don't overdo it. Gratuitousness waters down effectiveness. But a little profanity can enhance a story, or like Patton said, make statements stick. People remember funny sentences that have a little shock value. Profanity has a humorous quality to it, especially to teenagers. Even pastors use the occasional euphemism for a laugh.

It might be an unpleasant thing for many parents (like me) to accept, but our teenagers live in a world where profanity has become mainstream. From their jokes to their music, the occasional swear is a part of their language, whether we like it or not.

I say all of that to say this. Profanity as an emotional response to adversity is the adult version of a tantrum. It's a Civilian response. A Warrior response is action-oriented, not a knee-jerk complaint. Language reflects the soul. And *how* someone speaks (verbally or with their body language) in pressure situations is often an indicator as the kind of person they are.

In our program, we want our language during competition to mirror the core values of our Warrior Culture and the values of our institution. We don't tolerate cursing on the basketball court. Not because of a personal moral stance, but because of the school we represent and the Warriors we want to be. So, we intentionally practice self-control with language in the heat of battle. The ability to exercise self-control in our speech will be useful in our adult lives. We may as well work on this now, so when we go out in a diverse world, we'll have had some practice.

There is another reason why we don't allow our players to cuss on the court. I doubt fans watching a high school team with players spouting profanity left and right would come to the conclusion that they'd just watched a bunch of tough kids play. They're more likely to leave thinking those kids were out of control, over-emotional, immature, punks, or disrespectful. That's not the image a team of Warriors wants to portray.
When our players understand this. They're more likely to see *why* they should watch their mouth.

Most of them don't live in a world free of profanity. So instead of a moral stance on the societal constructs that are curse words. We take a practical approach.

I've tried both ways, the morality approach was far less effective.

ARTICULATING OUR WHY

"You are here today for three reasons. First, because you are here to defend your homes and your loved ones. Second, you are here for your own self-respect, because you would not want to be anywhere else. Third, you are here because you are real men, and all real men like to fight. When you here, every one of you, were kids, you all admired the champion marble player, the fastest runner, the toughest boxer, the big league ball players, and the All-American football players."
—General George Patton, US Army, June 5, 1944

Patton understood his men. He knew their *why* and just in case they had forgotten, he reminded them seconds into his speech. Some athletes know why they play. Most even know why they started playing. But so many, somewhere along the way, after hours working on their games, countless tedious drilling, the stress of living up to external and internal expectations, or multitudes of other reasons, they've forgotten why they play. Or at least haven't thought about their *why* in a very long time.

A skilled leader is not only a teacher of new ideas, but a reminder of old, forgotten ones. One of the best things a coach can do is get our players to remember their *why*. And if a player has never thought about their *why*, or it has changed, we need to guide them in the conversation. Patton does this with a simple reminder. It's not coincidental that he opens his speech with the *why*.

A strong *why* will dictate the tenacity and resilience in which we pursue excellence in a craft.

WINNING IS IMPORTANT

"Americans love a winner. Americans will not tolerate a loser. Americans despise cowards. Americans play to win all of the time. And I wouldn't give a hoot in hell for a man who lost and laughed. That's why Americans have never lost and will never lose a war. For the very idea of losing is hateful to an American."

—General George Patton, US Army, June 5, 1944

Athletes are one of the most competitive sub-groups in society. They were born that way. If we look at the leadership in competitive business, there is a direct correlation between business success and athletics.

According cnbc.com,[4] a disproportionate number of CEO's in the U.S. played sports when they were young. And the number is especially high for women. A study by Ernst and Young, of 821 high-level female executives surveyed, 90% played sports.

---

[4]   www.cnbc.com/amp/2017/01/11/want-to-be-a-ceo-later-play-sports-now.html

Winning is important. And it's important to our players. They don't want to hear that it doesn't matter. They want to play for a coach that wants to win as bad as they do, or more. When a player hears someone downplay the importance of winning, what they hear is a person giving themselves an out. They hear justification for failure. And the most competitive players are NOT okay with that. They get pissed because winning is important to them, and they won't hear otherwise. Worse, they might lose respect, and at that point, a coach has lost them.

In a Warrior Culture, winning is not the end-all-be-all. The value of failure, and the process are important because Warriors have the bigger picture in mind. But just because winning *is* important, too, doesn't minimize these things. It's not one or the other. It's all in one.

Want to enhance culture? Win. Everything will level up naturally.
Want to have culture problems? Lose.
Want to see culture collapse? Lose a lot.
Losing isn't fun, especially prolonged losing stretches. People are more likely to jump ship or mutiny when they believe it's sinking. That sucks, but it's the truth.

With this in mind, **scheduling is very important to program building.** When I took the job at Boyd in 2018, I scheduled our first 7 games against teams we would be favored over. We started 7-0.
Winning is a big deal.

Facing The Fear

"Death must not be feared. Death, in time, comes to all men. Yes, every man is scared in his first battle. If he says he's not, he is a liar. Some men are cowards, but they fight the same as brave men, or they get the hell slammed out of them, watching men fight who are just as scared as they are. The real hero is the man who fights even though he is scared. Some men get over their fright in a minute under fire. For some it takes an hour. For some it takes days. But a real man will never let his fear of death overpower his honor, his sense of duty to his country, and his innate manhood."
—General George Patton, US Army, June 5, 1944

Facing the fear is one of the most important aspects of Warrior Culture. For athletes, it means overcoming the fear of failure to compete to the best of your ability. We watch this play out in different ways during tournament time every year.

Experienced players, specifically seniors, often fall victim to Fear Of The End (FOTE). When they know the end is near, they see all their work and passion they've poured into their games being minimized to a few weeks, or even one night. That's a lot of pressure. The fear of their career being over (the athletic death) can cripple their performance if a player hasn't thought through why they are feeling this pressure.

Inexperienced players tend to fall victim to a Fear Of Messing Up (FOMU) mindset. Why? They've never done it in public when the stakes were this high. The first step to confidence is preparation (skill mastery) and the next step is public performance. Until they have performed well under the bright lights of the big stage (multiple times), true confidence can waver. That's okay, it's part of the process. Early in my coaching career, FOMU in big games was frustrating because I didn't recognize the source of the problem or help our players in any way. Instead, I labeled them.

"[Insert player's name] just isn't clutch."
or...
"She freezes in the big moment."
or...
"We just don't close out games."

Well, have we talked about it with those players? Or do we just whine about it to our spouses and assistants, effectively giving up on them, labeling them?

If we don't start getting in their heads to help them understand themselves and solve their "clutch" problems, we are doomed to see these problems repeated. Nobody can solve problems they don't know exist. As coaches, we have seen this play out enough to know how common this feeling is, especially in passionate, high IQ players.

When I was an assistant for Tommy Brown at Lee University, we used to joke about how we'd rather have the 60% free throw shooter who has the perfect amount of *I don't care* at the free throw line in the big moment, rather than the 80% shooter who cares too much and understands the pressure of the situation.

I heard an old coach say once, "Give me a dumb guy at the line in the clutch every time. Dumb guys don't realize the gravity of the moment."

Many of us have lived it in our own careers and regret lingers into our adult lives. If only we knew then what we know now.

Well, why don't we address it with our players before they find themselves in a mental space that causes them to freeze up in the big moment? Encourage them to embrace the fact that their career will end, and there is nothing they can do about it. Even if it ends with a win in a state championship game, the death of the career still happens.

Most high school players, even the cocky ones, don't think about such fears until they find themselves suffocating during the biggest tournament games. Coaches call it the "big eyes" or "deer in the headlights." And if a player finds themselves with this paralyzing feeling in a big moment of a tournament elimination game, it's often too late. The damage is done.

However, we can get ahead of it and be proactive. Part of being the captain of the ship is acknowledging the icebergs, even the unavoidable ones.

Proactivity implies taking immediate responsibility for the healthy headspace for our players.

Coaches can guide their players to a headspace that frees them up to play with liberated looseness. A headspace where the joy of competition trumps their fear of failure. We can accept our role as sports psychologists (an understated aspect of coaching) and attempt to solve the problem.

The Warrior Spirit is always growing, becoming, and changing for the better. As the champions of our Warrior Culture, it's on us to cultivate and nurture the minds of our Warriors. Not to label them as chokers, but to recognize the probability of fear creeping in and help them accept and overcome it when the time comes.

Like Patton did in this speech, embrace the reality of fear. Let them know they aren't alone. Then give them a picture of what a Warrior's death looks like. And do it *before* they go to battle and find themselves in the fire.

Inevitability is neither negative nor positive. It's an objective fact. The narrative of inevitability as a negative can be flipped to the positive so we can rise above fear and compete at our best in spite of it. Instead talking about not going out, what if we talked about how we are gonna go out. Fighting valiantly. Gloriously.

The tricky part for athletes is that many haven't considered the death of their season, or career, as inescapable until it's too late. And that will adversely affect their performance. **Facing fear head on is the best way to overcome it.**

In every state association, the unfortunate truth is that every team's season will end in failure and disappointment except one special group that rides a perfect wave of talent, chemistry, and lucky breaks to a gold ball. The rest end in despair.

But does it have to be despair? A Warrior knows that death comes to us all, and in that acceptance, finds newfound freedom. It is this freedom that enables magnificent last performances worth celebrating. **The grand finale to every Warrior's journey is glorious death in combat.**

THE MAGNIFICENCE OF COMPETITION

"Battle is the most magnificent competition in which a human being can indulge. It brings out all that is the best, and it removes all that is base."
— General George Patton, US Army, June 5, 1944

Sports are strange if we really think about it. Why do people get so worked up about these games? What makes them different from Monopoly or Hide and Seek? Strip away the human elements we love like emotion, camaraderie, pride, human error, and so on, and we're left with basic rules and logistics.

Take basketball, for instance. There is a ball, a floor with lines on it, two metal hoops with plexi-glass backboards, and two teams of 8 to 15 young people. Only 5 players on each team get to play at a time. The rest wait patiently for their turn. Some do not even get a turn. The 5 players on one team bounce the ball on the floor and pass it to each other in an effort to throw it in the hoop.

They do this while the other team tries to keep them from accomplishing this goal. Each team takes turns with the ball. They do this while constantly being yelled at by adults in their Sunday best. Other adults dressed in striped shirts are paid money to make sure the game is fair. The family, friends, and fans of the players pay money to watch the game.

During the game, the paying spectators feel that because they have spent money on the game itself, they're entitled to yell at everyone from the striped shirt rule enforcers, to the people in suits, to the players—usually their own children but sometimes other people's children—and anyone else they feel inclined to yell at.

Before the games, the players endure hours upon hours of demanding physical and mental preparation, often waiting in lines to do painful exercises like run or throw their bodies on the hardwood floor. All to throw the ball through the hoop more times than the teams they play. We're all weird. But we know there's something else to it.

It's not the games themselves that make us so passionate about them. It's how these games have evolved into art forms over the years. Art imitates life, and life imitates art. The fun, the challenges, the competitive atmospheres, the relationships we develop, and the opportunity for personal growth make sports more than games. They are not life and death, but the best simulation available to us. In its highest form, competitive sport *"brings out all that is the best, and it removes all that is base."*

Sports are practice for life. That's why we get so worked up about it.

THE SMALL WHYS

"All through your Army careers, you men have bitched about what you call chickenshit drilling. That, like everything else in the Army, has a definite purpose. That purpose is alertness. Alertness must be bred into every soldier."
— General George Patton, US Army, June 5, 1944

Most coaches love practice in the same way players love the games. We are prepared, in control, and on stage. But we must accept that players rarely feel as enthusiastic about practice as we do. It's *our* game, the place we feel most useful. Their game is *the* game.

I remember seeing Allen Iverson's notorious "practice" press conference when I was a college player in 2002. I was watching it with my dad (who was also my coach). Dad's immediate response, from his coaching lens, was the opposite perspective I had through my player's lens. He hated Iverson's words, and understandably so. But I felt like, *finally, somebody said it.*

I understood practice was important, but as a 21-year-old man who spent hours on the practice floor, doing the same drills week after week, month after month, and year after year, I could relate to Iverson's sentiment.

Practice can become a monotonous drag for players, through no fault of the coach. Most coaches do an outstanding job keeping things as competitive and fresh as they can, but there are some things that must be drilled and emphasized daily to implement strong fundamental habits and alertness in the whole team.

The more experience players have in the program, the more these drills bore them. But just because it's not accommodating the oldest, best player's immediate needs, doesn't mean that it's not something the team needs, especially the younger players who haven't formed the habits being drilled yet. These drills are a necessary evil.

It's important that we explain why we the tedious drills we do, just like Patton did in his speech. We should also talk to our older players separately to generate more buy in because they undeniably influence the mood of the locker room.

Just because they are bored, and these repetitive drills don't seem necessary for *their* development from a habit and skill standpoint, doesn't mean they can't level up in other areas and grow through these drills. They need to consider getting over their initial thoughts on an old drill to work on a different aspect of their game like communication and leadership.

Encourage the older players who may be bored with such drills to become coaches. At Lee and at Boyd, we gave upperclassmen players opportunities to enhance their communication skills by coaching from the sideline.

Take a common defensive shell drill for instance. Most programs do a variation of this drill. In our program, our players create the habit of flying to the perfect position with no hesitation on every pass. We must stay in a stance and move together as one unit. Once in position, our hands must be active, and our mouths must efficiently communicate our defensive responsibility to our teammates.

Our experienced guys know these points of precision like the back of their hand, so we allow them to demonstrate first. The younger players watch the way they move and the standard they set with their effort.

After their short demonstration, they each get to coach a younger player through the drill, constantly shouting reminders and praising effort that meets the standard. We've had special teams who got to the point where our coaches didn't have to coach much. We just blew the whistle to signal the transitions. Sometimes, we blew a longer whistle to stop the action and ask an older player to teach a concept that the young ones are failing to perform consistently.

This tactic has been effective for our programs. As Dawson Trotman once said, "Thoughts disentangle themselves when they pass through the lips and fingertips." When our players teach and perform, they will be on a higher plane of understanding.

We all know that we need to keep practices as competitive as possible, but regarding the tedious but necessary drilling, our players need to understand the *why* behind it. We need to tell them, let them tell others, and then get creative to keep them engaged and improving. Because, to the player, "We talkin' 'bout practice, man. Not a game. Practice."

THE POWER OF "WE ARE" LANGUAGE

"We have the finest food, the finest equipment, the best spirit, and the best men in the world."
— General George Patton, US Army, June 5, 1944

Patton's language is precise and purposeful here. The late 19th century American philosopher William James said, "As you think, so shall you be."
He also said, "If you want a quality, act as if you already have it."

In our Warrior Culture, we believe our self-talk will dictate our actions. We don't want to be tough or strive to be tough. **WE ARE tough.** A player doesn't think, *I'd like to be a great teammate.* They think, ***I AM a great teammate.***

These statements imply ownership of desirable character qualities. They engage a sense of responsibility and do wonders for a player's positive sense of self. A coach can model this with his speech. By saying, "...we have the best spirit, and the best men in the world." Patton is implanting pride, ownership, responsibility, and belief in the hearts and minds of his men. He is also displaying supreme confidence in the men under his command.
Confidence is contagious... and powerful.

Every Man Plays a Vital Role

"All of the real heroes are not storybook combat fighters either. Every single man in this Army plays a vital role. Don't ever let up. Don't ever think that your job is unimportant. Every man has a job to do, and he must do it. Every man is a vital link in the great chain."
— General George Patton, US Army, June 5, 1944

It is important to note that not all Warriors become famous. Not all athletes on a great team of Warriors will be featured in the local newspaper. Only one will lead the team in scoring. And a handful will be mentioned. But every player on the team who acts like a Warrior, no matter how small their role, needs to be noticed.

It may be one who goes after every rebound. Or the one who guards the other team's best player every night. Or the one who brings contagious spirit every day. And what about the kid who shows up to practice every day, knowing they aren't in the rotation, but works hard just to push the player who gets the lion's share of the playing time?

We cannot leave them nameless. Their name may not be in the paper... yet. But it must roll off our tongues often. If something is important to the fabric of our team, it needs to be recognized, or it might go away.

We need to celebrate the players who do the things that go unnoticed by the common fan. Every member of a Warrior Culture needs to believe that their work has meaning. They are there for a reason. As Patton said, *"Every man is a vital link in the great chain."* Their role is important. They need a name. And as coaches, it's up to us to notice. Give that Warrior a name.

I'M PROUD OF YOU

"You all know how I feel. I'll be proud to lead you wonderful guys in battle anytime, anywhere. That is all."
— General George Patton, US Army, June 5, 1944

Think back to when you were a child. And the person you admired the most—maybe your mother or father—said these words, "I'm proud of you." Sit in that headspace for a minute. Try to remember your feelings.

I can still feel my heart swell with pride and joy when I remember the times my dad said that to me. I'm forty, and last season my dad told me how proud he was of me and our team. It still hit me the same as it did when I was a child. Like the Grinch, my heart grew three sizes that day.

If we are proud of the people our players are becoming and the way they're conducting themselves, they *need* us to tell them. If we have earned their respect, we can't underestimate their desire to make us proud. Of course, we want them to be proud of themselves, but that's not always enough for them. They want us to be proud of them, too.

Most high school kids love their parents, but most athletes would say they have two sets of parents (especially those from single parent homes). They have the parents at home they were given and the parent at school they chose.

Affirmation and praise have a motivating effect on young people. Our players who are passionate about the sport we coach chose us. When we are proud of them, let's not keep it a secret. When we tell them, we inspire them to do more. And we make them smile, and that's as cool as it gets.

Chapter 2

Our Bushido Code

I've seen a lot of different locker room décor over the years, ranging from low-budget minimalist to extravagant luxury spaces to billboard-type reminders of culture.

As a person who prefers a T-shirts to trendy clothing, my preference is minimalist. Maybe that's because I attended schools that didn't have money in the budget for the finer things like new couches or spacious, neon-lit lockers. We had metal folding chairs, chalkboards, and una-showers. I get the appeal though.

When I was a player, I took an unofficial college recruiting visit. The coaches took me on a tour of the campus. It was nice, especially the athletic facilities. They showed me the locker room. There were fancy signs circling the entire space. And it was a big space, so we're talking around 15 to 20 signs. On each sign, there was a word with a command under it.
Like this...

SELF-CONTROL
We will display self-control at all times

The next one said...

DISCIPLINE
We will exercise discipline in all we do

The next one said...

RESPECT
We will respect our coaches, teammates, and opponents

And on and on and on... That may have been the day I began loathing motivational posters.

Then I saw my name on a locker. On the wooden stool inside it, a binder. Written on it, "THE BOBCAT WAY."[5] The assistant coach picked it up. "That's for you," he said.

It was thick. 150+ pages of core values, team rules, plays, and even details about the team's strength and nutrition plan. It looked like homework. And felt like school. I was 18 and enjoyed basketball and school being separate entities.

I put on my gear and went back into the gym to play pickup with their current players. On the way up, my dad told me to ask the players questions because they

---

[5] Okay, if your team mascot is the Bobcats, don't get offended. It's not you. I made that name up. It wasn't really the Bobcats.

are more likely to be truthful about the program than the coaches during a recruiting visit.

So after the first game, I asked one of them, "What's it like to play here?"

"It's aight," he said.

"Do you like it?"

"It's aight."

"Are you glad you came here?"

"I guess. It was my only option."

He didn't seem interested in elaborating, and I was nervous anyway, so I didn't press it. I may not be the smartest guy, but I'm not an idiot. He obviously had no interest in this conversation.

After playing for 45 minutes. I felt like I was just getting warmed up. 4 of the players disappeared between games. I started counting because I wanted to keep playing. In my home gym, we rarely stopped playing pickup before two hours in. 1, 2, 3, 4, me, and a 6th gave us enough for 3 on 3. But the 6th was taking off his shoes.

One assistant yelled, "Tim, you done?"

"Yeah, coach. I'm tired and have to work on a project tonight."

One of their best guards volunteered to be done so we could play 2 on 2. We played one game. It lasted maybe 5 minutes. The rest of them went to the locker room and left. Salty, I shot by myself for another 20 minutes. We talked to the coaches a little more, then drove home.

On the three-hour drive, I flipped through the binder. I just wanted to play basketball and learn on the court, not read a doctoral dissertation on how we were going to be good at playing basketball. Honestly, the binder said some good stuff. It painted a comprehensive (understatement) picture of a great program.

But the biggest problem I had with the entire ordeal, is that there was nothing about playing in their environment that day that mirrored anything that binder claimed about their culture. It was a wordy waste of paper and ink, and the signs on the walls of the locker room were nothing more than chic sports décor.

Maybe I caught them on a bad day. Maybe there were too many rules and values to put a premium on any. Maybe it was window dressing for recruits. I'm not sure. But I know this—there was a better chance of me swimming naked to Antarctica than me going to school there.

The Warrior Way

The Samurai in Japan are viewed by many as one of the greatest Warrior Cultures in world history. The misunderstood aspect about the Samurai is that they were not all Warriors, but they were all aristocrats. One didn't become a Samurai because they were a noble Warrior. They had to be born into a certain class of family. Samurai status was inherited, not earned. But they had a standard, a code, and they were serious about it.

If a Samurai fell out of favor with their masters or brought dishonor to their clan in some way, they were required to commit ritual suicide (Seppuku) to keep their honor. The stakes were quite high. Some dishonored Samurai refused to perform Seppuku and became Ronin, which means wanderer or drifter. Ronin Samurai would fight in duels, and many, similar to Ninja Warriors, would turn to mercenary life.

The Samurai were artists, business owners, politicians, and yes... some soldiers. And regardless of their employment or status in Samurai culture, they were Warriors. Especially Miyamoto Musashi, the master swordsman, strategist, and philosopher whose words of wisdom we will quote often in this book.

It was not the actions of Samurai that influenced great Warrior Cultures that came after them. It was their wisdom—The Bushido Code.

The word is translated from the Japanese word *Bushi* meaning *Warrior*. And *Do* meaning *Way*.

Tenets of the Bushido Code:

GI—Integrity
REI—Respect
YU—Heroic Courage
MEIYO—Honor
JIN—Compassion
MAKOTO—Honesty and Sincerity
CHU—Duty and Loyalty

The brilliance of the Bushido Code is its simplicity. It's short and to the point. Yet abstract enough that we can apply these virtues to enhance our modern lives. If a person lives their life by the Bushido Code, they will have lived well—with honor.

Honor in life and death meant everything to the Samurai which is why this code still stands as one of the great instruction manuals for living well in human history.

Our Code (Core Values)

I never forgot that recruiting trip and the bulky 3-ring-bound collection of coaching clinic gold masquerading as a program manual. I remember how the signs in the locker room were in stark contrast with the culture of the pickup games. I remember the abundance of whining about calls and the lack of overall competitiveness.

I don't want this to appear judgemental of another coach. It's not. Looking back, I know this coach knew more about basketball and coaching a team than me, a player. But the player's perspective and perception matter.

It's important to have core values for our programs. But with this story in mind, we should think about how we can frame these values in a way most likely to generate total buy-in from our players. Not only buy-in, but passion.

How can we get them to be as passionate about our values as our coaching staff is? That may be impossible, but our challenge every year is to see how tightly we can close this gap. Here's some ideas that have worked best for us.

KEEP THE CODE CONCISE

Too much information can overwhelm our players. The focus should be narrow in our wording, but broad enough to influence a wide range of our behaviors. At Boyd, we have four core values that dictate all of our actions.

1—Get better every day.

"Study strategy over the years and achieve the spirit of the Warrior. Today is victory over yourself yesterday: Tomorrow is your victory over lesser men."

—Miyamoto Musashi

Our emphasis on daily improvement doesn't just apply to basketball, but our mindset and actions off the court as well. From the classroom, to our relationships, to the court, personal growth is the first staple of our Warrior Way.

We want to be better tomorrow than we were yesterday. And better tomorrow than we are today. That is the daily battle the Warrior fights.

2—Toughness.

To be in our program, toughness is not a suggestion, it's a requirement. It is physical and mental. These two aspects of toughness go hand in hand. It's often said that toughness is 90% mental and 10% physical.[6] I appreciate the sentiment, but I'd argue that arbitrary stats can be misleading.

We can't have physical toughness without mental toughness, and vice versa. That doesn't mean we have to be the biggest, strongest, or fastest, but pushing ourselves physically strengthens the mind so we can push through walls of fatigue.

Sometimes, the mind wants to go, but the body says no. Our goal is to do everything within our power to be in the kind of shape that allows our minds to push the limits our bodies impose on us.

When our players are in great shape, they realize that their minds can push their bodies further than they thought possible. If we aren't in great shape, our mental fortitude will be significantly handicapped.

So, we put a premium on the weight room and conditioning so our players can go harder and longer than our opponents. Performing difficult physical tasks give us the ability to channel the power of the mind.

---

[6] Buying into vague stats that have obviously been made up on the spot can be a dangerous game to play when it comes to pushing the limits of the body. The body speaks to the mind for a reason.

The most important aspect of toughness for our program is our perseverance in the face of adversity. It's our resilience.

3—Be a great teammate.

"Think lightly of yourself and deeply of the world."
—Miyamoto Musashi

In basketball, team chemistry is a critical component of winning. A cornerstone requirement for our players to be great teammates will influence our relationships from the way we speak to each other to suppressing petty jealousy to celebrating each other's successes. We want to be pure hearted. And that means each team member has the emotional maturity necessary to celebrate the successes of their teammates without being threatened by them. We must speak clearly about this because the battle for the purity of young athletic minds is constant.

Not an acceptable teammate, or even a good teammate. We are going for great. And great all the time. If successful, the level of respect we have each other will be high.

4—Have fun.

We prioritize fun to the point that we've made it a core value. Our players started playing because the game was fun. We want an environment that maximizes our enjoyment of our team experience.

We only get to do this together once. Might as well have a great time. I've found the more fun our players have, the looser they are, and the better they perform.

In our programs, core values based on character (how we want to act) rather than hard-and-fast rules have served us well. Values accomplish two things in the hearts of our players—Inspiration and impulse control. Rules work for impulse control, but they aren't likely to inspire permanent behavior.

Players are going to mess up. They may be repentant and have a great heart. They may not Every situation is unique. Every player's personality is distinct. And often, our judgement needs a little wiggle room.

It takes contemplation, good judgement, and high character to be confident in this area. We have to make tough calls every tryout, practice, and game, so we should trust our experience. The best coaches I've been around don't tie their hands with rules. But they have the courage to make situational decisions based on their core values and stand by them. And I'm not alone in feeling this way.

"Too many rules get in the way of leadership. They just put you in a box... People set rules to keep from making decisions... Leadership is ongoing, flexible, and dynamic. As such, leaders have to maintain a certain amount of discretion."

—Coach K

Culture Shouldn't Feel Like Homework

High school athletes have enough school work. The term *student of the game* doesn't hold the same weight with your average player as it does with coaches. Players want to play. They want to learn, improve, and be prepared, but the vast majority DO NOT want more schooling on top of the school they already have. Even the appearance of an extra-curricular activity resembling school work can have a negative effect on some of our players.

A coach might say, "Our players need to be students of the game." While this sentiment may be correct, for every player who buys into this "student of the game" mentality,[7] there will be ten who have no desire to be studious about sports. They actually dread the idea. The last thing we need is for our players to dread film sessions because they burned out on the studious tactics we used in our culture building process.

Core values are best implemented, practiced, and reinforced in action (workouts, practices, and games) rather than theory (classrooms and notebooks). I used to reject this idea because I appreciated the value of being a "student of the game" as a player.

But I was the son of a coach who chose coaching as a profession, and there is no doubt in my mind that my predisposition for coaching had a lot to do with my inclination to be studious about the game.

---

[7] And this player will probably become a coach one day.

In my second year of coaching, my dad said to me, "You'll never be a good coach until you accept that most of your players will be nothing like you."
I responded angrily, "Well, they should be. I know what wins."
He responded calmly, "That's fine, but it doesn't matter, and you've missed the point."

Fifteen years later, I got the point. Most players don't think like coaches. They think like players. It's more effective when we avoid cliché coach-speak and clinical teaching. That's how we (coaches) learn.

Most players learn best through experience. So, we need to consider teaching them where they are, the way they want to be taught, instead of the way we like to teach.

ON THE WALLS: WARRIOR IMAGES, NOT WORDS

A Warrior Culture celebrates doing instead of talking. Most athletes respond to visuals and pictures better than words, anyway. So we celebrate the Warriors we look up to. We recognize their names and faces. **It's symbolic. Our space inspires action.**

In our locker room, we have a framed picture of Arturo Gatti and Mickey Ward on the wall. And when our Warriors graduate, their image will go on that wall. We celebrate our Warriors. And if our players want to be on that wall, they know they must stay on the path.

ACCOUNTABILITY

It is the responsibility of the coach to create a culture of accountability. Failure to live up to our Warrior way by violating core values must be called out every time. Consistency is key.

There's a lot of chatter in coaching circles about player-led teams vs. coach-led teams. The common consensus is we need to have player-led teams instead of coach-led teams.

When I was in college, I had a professor who had a great impact on my thought processes. On the first day of class, he said, "Truth never fears a challenge." That stuck with me. Ever since, I've tried to challenge nearly everything I've considered to be truth.

Truth can be complicated and pragmatic. With that in mind, I often ask this question over and over, "What if we've been wrong about that?" If we don't feel comfortable with questions like this, we won't grow much.

So, on this topic of the player-led team, can we really expect 15 to 18-year-old kids to be equipped the knowledge of leadership and life experiences necessary to lead our teams? To be in charge of their peers? And do they even want that?

I've found it rare that they do. Remember, we are talking about high school players (teenagers). Being liked and accepted by their peers is important to them. They often forget things and get lost in the social aspects of their day. Some of their parents even have a hard time getting them to make their bed every morning. And I'm not disparaging them, I'm just presenting the argument that it may not be fair for us to ask our teenage players to be the vocal and emotional leaders of our teams.

We may be asking too much. Maybe the one we're asking to step up and lead just wants to be led by someone objective and wise [Read: old].

Some may be ready to step up and lead, and those players will do it without being asked. But some are quiet and the thought of being vocal with their peers, especially calling them out, is terrifying.

Some don't have enough understanding of the game outside of their limited positional experience to lead others. Some want to lead, feel like they need to lead, may even try to lead, but they just need to shut up.

One of our best, most talented players at Lee was quiet. His name was Jerel. He worked hard every day, but it wasn't in his nature to be a vocal leader. So, he didn't say much. He just hooped and led by example.

He was as tough as they come, even playing most of his senior season with a fractured shooting hand. Everyone in our locker room appreciated him, but more importantly, everyone respected him.

There are two character flaws we won't deal with for long—selfishness and softness. If selfish or soft behavior continues, a player will no longer be a part of our team. There's no room for these behaviors in a Warrior Culture.

We never let anyone off the hook for weakness in these areas, even if it means calling each other on it from time to time. We can neither confirm nor deny that we've gotten into physical altercations during a few of these confrontations, but I can confirm that problems get solved. And self-awareness and self-correction are accomplished. And respect is earned. That's what friends are for, right?

Anyway, after a heated practice Jerel's senior year, one of his teammates whined in the locker room about how he was tired of Coach telling him he was soft. Jerel rarely spoke up. But when he did, his words carried significant weight.

He said, "If it hurts your feelings that Coach said you're soft, then you're probably soft. When Coach calls me soft, I laugh. I ain't getting my feelings hurt. If you know you ain't soft, why would it bother you? Maybe there's some truth to it. If you don't like that, stop being soft."

Mic drop. Conversation ender.

Sometimes the quiet ones are just waiting to say something profound. So maybe we should quit pushing them to talk so much all the time. Nobody wants to be who they are not.

A truism in a vacuum, when taken to the extreme in real world application, often becomes an absurdity. This is a common problem in our application of coaching theory. Just because it sounds great on paper, doesn't make it practical across all programs. The idea of a player-led team being a goal can be problematic as a one-size-fits-all idea. There are reasons the player-led team idea can be problematic in high school sports.

1—Are the players getting the leadership they need?

"The most important piece is that this team gets the leadership it needs. That's more important than where that leadership is coming from."

—Brian Kight

The vast majority of teams of teenagers need an older Alpha to lead them. Maybe once every decade, we may have a team of players who possess the capabilities and knowledge to lead at a high level, but the members of those teams are still teenagers with growing minds and teenage struggles. Even those teams need stable adult leadership when the storms of a season get rough.

2—Are we breeding resentment?

We may have a player that says all the right things to his/her peers, but at some point, peer preaching becomes a drag to those being preached to. And it can lead to resentment.

We want to eliminate resentment in our team culture, not create avoidable situations where resentment can fester. It's important to remember what it was like to be a teenager. The last thing a teenager needs or wants is to be preached at by a pious peer, especially in a publicly shaming way.

The information could be spot on, but remember, we can be right at the wrong time and be wrong. And we can be right, but be the wrong person to say it, and be wrong.

3—Are we deflecting responsibility for future failure?

If the standards of our culture are not upheld, who's responsibility is that? The players? So are we saying it's their job to lead the group? I thought that was our job.

When things don't work out the way we want, do we get angry and say it's their fault the standards haven't been upheld? If so, what are we even there for. To me, that sounds like an egregious example of finger-pointing, deflecting our responsibility.

This is the problem I have with coaches who adopt this ideology that claims the player-led team is the goal. We preach values like owning personal responsibility and controlling the controllable, but when it's our turn to own our leadership shortcomings, it's the fault of the players. They were supposed to lead their team.

In 2018, our first week of official practice at Boyd presented a challenge that made me put significant thought into this player-led team construct.

Early in the week, our defensive ineptitude was visceral. Our staff learned that our players didn't have a baseline of understanding regarding man to man defensive principles. Simple concepts like jumping to the ball on every pass and getting into a low defensive stance were new and far from habitual. We taught the same things over and over again during those first few weeks.

That wasn't the frustrating part. We expected that. The frustrating part was the way our players talked down to each other, calling their teammates out on mistakes the whistleblower would make on their next rep. On Friday of that first week, I'd had enough.

"For the next month, everyone in this gym that isn't a coach just needs to shut up. Listen, learn, and apply.

You're trying to teach things you don't understand yet. You're rolling your eyes at each other because you're making the same mistakes you just yelled at someone else for. I'd be rolling my eyes, too.

"We'll hold you accountable for the details right now. Let us do the coaching. Focus on your game. If you're talking, you should only be saying the job you're doing or encouraging a buddy. That's it. We'll re-evaluate this in a month when some of you've created good habits. And when you've learned how to talk to each other with some respect. Until then, shut up and listen."

The next month, after a lot of work, little verbal instruction from players, and a ton of learning, we had a few guys who had earned the right to give tactful reminders to their teammates.

As the coach, we need to be the benchmark, the ultimate Warrior of our culture, and it's our job to fight for our culture every day. And on our most special teams, we may develop smart, mature players who will champion our culture with us—side by side.

Our players will speak the truth with grace in such a way that it's likely to be heard and accepted by their peers. They will command such respect that their teammates would be pained to let them down. They might embody our core values and be as passionate about them as we are.

But even the best Warriors on our team will still need us to lead them. So maybe we should adjust our expectations and demands with the player-led team idea. If we rejected the term *player-led* and changed it to *player-inclusive*, our perspective and approach might be more balanced and dynamic, instead of ideological.

We have found that by giving our players a voice, instead of forcing them to police values, has allowed their relationships within our team to be more like productive partnerships, instead of condescending dictatorships. They have a voice that isn't threatening and likely to be heard.

APPLICATIONS OF PLAYER INCLUSIVE LEADERSHIP

Pregame—If we are playing a team for the second time, I'll let players give the scouting report on the player they will guard. We have instructed them in previous practices, so they aren't just going by the memory of the last game. They are usually spot on. It's likely that they are more locked in during that week's practices because they might be called on in the pregame scout.

Half time evaluation and adjustments—Player feedback at half time is valuable. During a normal ten-minute half time break, I meet with the staff for a minute or two, giving the players a chance to talk to each other on their own.

Then when our staff comes in, I always say the same thing, "What did you see?" Way more often than not, they have seen something valuable that our coaching staff missed.

In 2018, we were less experienced. Sometimes they said something (always concise), and sometimes they had no idea what had happened. One year later in 2019, we had five experienced seniors, who had a thorough grasp of our system and values. They were more confident and had a better vision of the dynamics of each game. They got better at articulating their thoughts with confidence. Sometimes, I'd let them go for two or three minutes. Most of the time they were spot on, and all I had to do was bring it home, giving a little more clarity, a few reminders, and specific adjustments. And how those things would lead to a win.

I'm sure you're thinking, *That sounds like a player led team.* Yes, I guess it does. But that's five experienced seniors who were a once in a decade type team. But even that team needed the half time conversation to be redirected to the most relevant points.

The most helpful dialogues have a Joe Rogan-style moderator who makes sure the main things remain the main things. We have to be the Joe Rogan of our locker room to make sure these half time conversations aren't derailed. We still have to lead this talk. Remember, leadership is flexible and dynamic.

CORE VALUES MIRRORING PERSONALITY

For maximum authenticity and passion, coaches need to consider the values that mean the most to them. For us, it's a growth mindset, resilience, and relationships. Thus, our core values mirror these traits we are most passionate about—Get better every day, be tough, and be a great teammate. We must believe our sermons in the core of our souls.

We've seen it countless times—Belichick's team is cool and calculated, Les Miles's team competes like wild animals, Bob Huggins's team is the meanest bunch in the country, Roy Williams's team looks like they're having a ton of fun. Teams naturally take on the personality of their coach.

Our example is our most powerful teaching tool. And our authenticity as the champion of our culture is paramount because trust is a prerequisite for influence. Kids are smart and will smell a fraud like a police dog sniffs out drugs in an airport suitcase. Work dogs live for their jobs. They love to do what they've been bred to do.

And there are kids who feel like it's their job to question authority. For one reason or another, some of them tragic, these kids have an actual reason for their skepticism toward adult authority figures.

They've been burned before. Many have been hurt, abused, neglected, and lied to by the very people supposed to love them. These kids relish in the opportunity to uncover fraudulent behavior in adults. It reinforces their skeptical worldview and fuels the rebellion they feel deep down.

No matter how we feel about teenagers with a rebellious lean, they exist. And a few might be in our locker rooms without us even realizing it.

I relate to these kids, which compels me to address how imperative it is that we give them a tangible reason to believe in the goodness and altruism that humanity, at its best, can be. We need to, as Gandhi would say, "be the change" they desperately need in their lives.

For the older ones, we may be their last chance for hope. If we, as mentors, fail them, and they go out into the harsh world as jaded adults, a lifetime of personal growth could become nearly impossible to attain. This sounds like a worst-case scenario, but I would bet that it's more common than we might think.

We must model our Bushido Code every day, striving for consistence in our every word, action, and reaction. We won't be perfect. We will fail, but **our failure should be an anomaly, not the norm.**

When we fail to live up to our code, we have to own it. This isn't a disconnect with our players. In fact, it has the opposite effect.

Kids know people aren't perfect. What bothers them isn't failure, and definitely not admission of failure, but projecting perfection. It makes them feel like they aren't good enough because they can't attain such perfection.

When they find out when person who has projected themselves as perfect, is just as fallible as they are, they might label them a liar or a fraud. This fraud may get away with it once or twice, but eventually, the teen police will bust him because his actions don't align with his words. At that point, any ability he had to influence is over.

A CULTURE OF ACKNOWLEDGEMENT

Want to see bad behavior repeated? Ignore it.
Want to see inconsistent behavior? Use physical punishment as motivation.
Want to see good behavior repeated? Acknowledge people. And celebrate the heck out of those behaviors.

Values mean a lot to coaches, so when we see them in action, it should ignite a positive emotional reaction. The more genuinely intense the celebration, the more a player will want to be on the receiving end of those celebrations. This is basic human nature, but man, I fall short here so often. So, again, I'm reminding myself. We love it when people clap for us. It just feels good.

PART 2:
Resilience

Bucs: GOOD.

"When things are going bad, there's gonna be some good that's gonna come from it... Unexpected problems—GOOD, we have the opportunity to figure out a solution. That's it. When things are going bad, don't get all bummed out. Don't get startled. Don't get frustrated. If you can say the word "GOOD", guess what, it means you're still alive. It means you're still breathing. And if you're still breathing, well then hell, you still got some fight left in you. So, get up, dust off, reload, recalibrate, re-engage, and go out on the attack."

—Jocko Willink

The U.S. Navy SEALs have a saying when things get difficult, "**GREAT.**"
American Civilians have a saying when things get difficult, "**GREAT.**"

The same word. Polar opposite meaning. To a SEAL, the word "GREAT" calls to action. Every failure is an opportunity to learn. Every obstacle is a challenge, and most problems can be solved tactically. If it can't, they'll exhaust every resource to before they throw in the towel. But SEALs don't throw towels in concession like a boxer would, their towel is a reassessment that finds an alternative approach toward solving the problem.

To your average American Civilian, uttering the word *great* in response to an obstacle is a sarcastic whine. We've all heard it said, and if we're being honest, have said it ourselves more than once.

The difference between the Warrior and the Civilian mindset is most obviously displayed in this simple word.

A guy named Paul played on the first team I ever coached. He was talented, could really shoot it, and was easily the toughest player I've ever coached. He could be difficult to coach because he had zero tolerance for softness in his teammates. That sounds like good thing, and it is until you've had your fill of breaking up fights in practice. But even though he was a chore at times, I loved that side of him. And he's one of my favorite people I've ever coached because of his toughness.

Predictably, when Paul's college basketball career ended, he went to BUD/s. to become a SEAL. Eight years ago, Paul spoke to coaches about his SEAL team's response to adversity at our week-long team camp at Lee. He let us in on the power of "GREAT."

The next day, I watched these coaches share this attitude with their players. As I reffed game after game, I heard the word over and over. Hustle went up. Pouting went down. Communication went up because the players were challenged to get over their feelings when they heard one ultra-concise piece of coaching—"GREAT." And the biggest winner was their on-court performance. The players loved it.

Jocko Willink let the world in on the SEAL "GOOD" attitude in his book, *Extreme Ownership*[8], and he

---

[8] Willink, Jocko, and Leif Babin. *Extreme Ownership*. St. Martin's Press, 2015

articulated the idea perfectly on his podcast. For those fortunate enough to hear the message and apply the mindset, their lives have been changed for the better.

Paul had told us his SEAL team's word was "GREAT." One can speculate about why the word became "GOOD" when Jocko brought it to the masses. Maybe his team actually said, "GOOD." Maybe the word needed to change to "GOOD", before it was brought to Civilian masses who misuse the word *great* to fit their complaining mentality. Either way, "GOOD" can't be misunderstood in this context.

I showed our Boyd Buchanan Bucs Jocko's "GOOD" video on YouTube. It was the introduction to our core value of toughness. Almost instantly, our kids became obsessed with the mindset. The word meant everything to us. It echoed off the walls at practice. We hashtagged it on the tweets of our game results. We ordered plain black shooting shirts with one word across the front, "GOOD." And our attitude toward failure quickly went from one of complaining and quitting to problem solving and pushing forward.

Our players wanted to be Warriors. They wanted to be tough. They wanted to possess the will of a winner. With the "GOOD" mindset, they were learning how.

Resilience: an ability to recover from or adjust easily to misfortune or change.
That definition could indict many athletes and coaches on soft civilian charges. It's convicted me at

times. But that's the beauty of life. "Every passing minute is another chance to turn it all around."[9]

With our kids, that sentence has never been more true. One day—laying down on a Friday night in football. The next—leaving it all on the floor in basketball, fighting like Warriors, and getting up on a mission every time they were knocked down.

Resilience is a gift inside us, but we have to accept it by being honest, self-aware, and courageous in our inner monologue. Sometimes, the ego has to be broken first. But with no exceptions, our feelings about obstacles and failure need be flipped.

"There is nothing outside of yourself that can ever enable you to get better, stronger, richer, quicker, or smarter. Everything is within. Seek nothing outside of yourself."
—Miyamoto Musashi

Resilience is built when we learn from failure. Resilience is impeded when emotion negates what we could have learned from failure.

Honestly, it was easy at Boyd. Our athletes were so beaten down by the previous football and basketball seasons, they were desperate to be inspired to become someone they could be proud of. Any ego they had before was a distant memory. They were blank slates.

---

[9] *Vanilla Sky*. Directed by Cameron Crowe, performances by Tom Cruise and Penelope Cruz, Paramount, 2001.

Ready to become who they wanted to be, they just needed to be taught. And held accountable.

That's the *Catch-22* about ego. We have to take pride in who we are and who we're becoming, but not the pride expressed by a *know-it-all* attitude. That is arrogance.

Another positive about failure is it's one of the best tools to keep ego in check. If we aren't careful, ego becomes another impediment to resilience because one loses the desire for mentorship. And when that happens to a high school or college athlete, the player's potential is capped. They don't improve at the rate they should. Growth is minimal, and in the worst cases, it ends. For life. Resilience requires mentorship. Players must want it. We must coach it.

It's not only the SEALs who believe the power of resilience is an integral part of a Warrior's character. It's a common denominator of every great Warrior Culture in human history.

Chapter 3

The Hard Stuff for Players

For centuries, an Amazonian tribe called the Satere-Mawe used a ritual to initiate their young men into Warriors of their clan. First, elders harvest local Bullet Ants known to have the most powerful sting in the world and then lace them into traditional gloves where they await the hands of would be Warriors. The Bullet Ant gets its name from the pain of its sting, where a single encounter rates as high as a bullet wound. It's also known as the 24-Hour Ant because of how long the pain takes to wear off. Or how long it takes someone who has had a bad reaction to die. These names are given in relation to one sting from one ant.

According to tradition, the ants are gathered and then sedated as the gloves are woven from local foliage. The ants are laced into the seams with their stingers pointed towards the inside of the gloves as the potential Warrior's hands are coated with a black charcoal dusting. The boy sticks out his arms as tribal elders take the gloves that look like palm frond oven mitts and place them over the boy's hands and wrists.

Upon insertion, the ants struggle to escape their newfound captivity. They work themselves into a frenzy, biting continuously over the next few minutes as the boy tries his best not to display any emotion of weakness. The goal is to keep the gloves on for minutes while fighting off the common side effects of burning, throbbing, nausea and all-encompassing pain. To throw off the gloves is to become a Nameless. To keep them on for the time limit is just the beginning.

Through the rest of the day and into the night, the young tribal member will fight off alternating fevers and chills, bouts of hallucinations and general misery with only the dream of becoming a tribal Warrior and the support of elders to get them through. If he makes it through the night, the good news is after those 24 hours, he is well on his way to becoming a Warrior.

According to formal Satere-Mawe tradition a young man must endure the ritual up to 20 times in the weeks and months leading up to his confirmation as a tribal Warrior.

And we think running sprints in a field on a hot day is hard.

There was only one country Alexander the Great saw but didn't try to conquer—Sparta. Even one of the greatest conquerors in world history knew better than to mess with this unhinged bunch. They were bad. And crazy. One has to be crazy to be that bad.

Estimates state that nearly half of Spartan male babies died of neglect or were murdered because, if they had a disability or any other weakness, they would be abandoned or killed by their parents. Literally, only the strongest survived, and then things got wild.

Spartan boys only lived under the care of their mothers until age 7, when they would live in military barracks and learn from Warrior teachers called wardens. The teachers would encourage fighting and hazing amongst the children. Even throwing them into the wild for periods of time, where the boys would have to use their most basic survival instincts. If a child misbehaved, the warden would beat him with a whip. Then he'd send the boy to his father, who'd beat him worse.

In Sparta, a male was a soldier. All other forms of education were banned. In the barracks, the boys were given the bare minimum of food for survival. They were encouraged to steal, but without getting caught. If caught, they'd get double whippings again.

They held annual festivals where spectators would gather in arenas to watch and place bets. One would have the hungry boys no-holds-barred fight over a block of cheese. Another festival was even more brutal. The boys would volunteer to be whipped in front of a crowd until they couldn't stand anymore. They wanted to prove they could take the pain longer than any other. It was a great honor to take part. And the greatest honor to be the last boy standing. Roman civilians caught wind of these events and started vacationing in Sparta so they could watch them. Romans were sick puppies.

The Spartan methods didn't teeter on the brink of madness. They dove head first into the pool of insanity. But Spartan men became the best Warriors the world has ever seen, even if by unnatural selection. Which affirms a common sentiment—to be the best, one might have to be a little crazy.

And we think lifting weights is hard.

Becoming a Warrior is no easy task. That's why it is so worthwhile. There are countless struggles, physical and mental, people must endure to develop the Warrior mentality.

The single most important coaching point in a Warrior Culture is resilience. This isn't a new idea. Warrior Cultures throughout history put their children through rites of passage before they would be considered worthy and capable members of their tribe. Some were extreme in their methods, but they understood *why* they did it.

Resilient people are the most likely to succeed. And in contrast, people who lack resilience will inevitably be crushed by the waves of challenge and suffering during their lives.

If the greatest Warriors in history placed a premium on resilience, we should take note and be intentional in developing resilience in our players. And in our own lives.

Membership in a Warrior Culture is not given in an instant. It's earned over time.

As a college player and later as a young coach I refereed summer basketball team camp games. It was a great way to pick up extra cash. One of my favorite things about officiating team camp games was the amount I could learn from coaches while they were in their element.

During one of these camp games, a team called the Wildcats from White Plains, Alabama, coached by Chris Randall, were getting trounced early. Normally, they were a good team. They played hard, were disciplined, and always had a baseline of toughness about them. A Warrior reputation. But this camp team on the court I worked was a mix of their A and B teams, and the point guard running the show was a B team sophomore trying to find his footing.

Of all the regular teams that came to our team camp, the Wildcats were one of the most well-coached. It was also the consensus of the officials that their games were the toughest to call because of how hard they played and how hard Chris coached. If you were calling his court, you'd better be on your toes.

"TIME OUT!" Coach Randall shouted. I blew the whistle, and his team sprinted to the sideline. I inched closer to their huddle. Every Wildcat but one had locked eyes on their coach, the point guard who knew the time out was for him. Immediately, Chris got after him.

"Look here. Look *up* at me!" The PG snapped his eyes up to his coach. "Listen, I got hard truth you gotta hear. You good with that?"

The PG nodded.

"Son, you can be slow." The PG was not the quickest.

"You can be short." The PG was not the tallest.

"You can be fat." The PG was not exactly trim.

"Heck, son, you can be any of those things and still find a way to contribute to this team but you *cannot* be soft."

The PG's eyes lit up. His body language told his coach he was heard. You know, that look you get when you've touched a kid's soul. Coach Randall is a master of those moments. His truth gets to the heart of his athletes and inspires them. He doesn't coddle them or sacrifice expectations. No Wildcat gets a free pass. The best part, none of them would want one. He can do this because he leaves no doubt that he loves them.

The PG flew back out onto the floor. He didn't play a perfect game from that point on, but he sure led his team in a way that would help them in the future. He also competed in a way that would make him a better player. Not only that, in a way he could be proud of later that night while enjoying a slice of cold pizza in the dorm with his boys.

After the game I caught up to Coach Randall and asked him about that timeout. He said, "Man, that kid could be a really good player. I gotta tell him the truth. Yes, he ain't built like a natural, but he can play if he really wants to. I can't make it easy for him because it ain't ever easy for kids who ain't that athletic. If I take him out of the game there, it's an easy out. He's gotta suck it up and sink or swim. Heck, I wanted *him* to see if he'd sink or swim out there. They get tougher when they gotta play through stuff."

This wasn't a new theme for the Wildcats. We've watched his teams at our camp every year for the last

20 years, and Chris is still doing his thing. They have varying talent every summer, but they bring the same culture. To be a Wildcat, you're expected to be tough. And you better guard.

Coach Randall brings middle school kids to team camp one week and high school athletes the next. And he runs around gym to gym coaching them all. By the time a player earns a spot on their varsity roster, he doesn't have to give many speeches prodding them to play harder. That hay goes in the barn before they get a varsity jersey. His players either become Warriors or weed themselves out.

Our 2019 Bucs played them in an absolute street fight. The first quarter ended 6-6. One might have thought it was a football game between two teams with bad kickers. You could count the uncontested shots on one hand. There weren't even many uncontested passes. Fans might have thought it was ugly, but a few people I know, who love to see teams get after it, thought it was High School D at its nastiest. Whatever it was, it was "A Heavyweight Fight." At least that's what the reporter covering the game called it.[10]

A place in a Warrior Culture should require more than just being talented enough to get a jersey. If we're tired of coaching kids that don't really want to be there, we should make it tougher to be there. That could be through off-season conditioning, GPA expectations, study hall requirements, or anything that's important to our culture.

---

[10] www.easportstoday.com/2019/11/27/a-heavyweight-fight/

Our players will do things they're coached to do. I know a coach who only assigns locker nameplates to his players after they've taken a charge in a game. His team takes a ton of charges. Go figure.

Do Hard Things

It would be hard to imagine a Satere-Mawe Warrior coming home from his first battle and complaining to his fellow villagers, "I wasn't prepared for that. It was too hard."

Our best scorer is going to get fouled the most in games. Sometimes, they won't get the calls. Are they used to playing through it? Have they gotten so good at playing through physicality that they don't need whistles to be successful?
Our best defender will get screened more than anyone else on the team. Often double-screened. Is it ok for them to say, "Coach, I got screened"?

Consistently competing at a high level is hard. But the more difficult we make our practices, the more we run toward challenges, the more we compete, and the more we emphasize personal responsibility, the easier consistency will be to attain.

Those bullet ants won't bite with less pain, but the Warrior just gets better at handling it. They get tougher. Calloused. Mean. Our teams need to be challenged in creative ways to keep them prepared.

Be Who We Are

> *"You must understand that there is more than one path to the top of the mountain."*
>
> —Miyamoto Musashi

Checking up on every little thing our players do is exhausting and unrealistic. And if we try to be good at a hundred things, we'll be great at nothing. Accountability is consistent reinforcement of what is most important to our team.

If making 3-point shots is a huge part of our offense, is it the focal point of skill work and are we tracking our makes in practice?
If keeping the ball out of the paint is central to our defensive scheme, is it still emphasized in scrimmages like it is in our defensive containment drills?

We can't be amazing at everything, but we can pick a handful of things and say, "This is what we're about." For some cultures, we may focus on the speed of our transition game. For others, it may be a stingy half-court defense. For a crazy Warrior Culture in the Amazon, it was a Bullet Ant glove.

If we choose to believe that people are doing the best with what they know, we'll find a new level of compassion for our players. And we'll be more likely to shoulder the responsibility for our communication.

If they aren't playing the way our culture requires, they may not be getting the message.

The most effective thing about Coach Randall pointing out hard truths to his fledgling point guard was that he left him an avenue to success that was completely in his control. In more concrete terms, it might look like showing a player on film when they do well as many times as we show them when they fall short.

The expectations of the Satere-Mawe Warrior are clear because it's tribal even to go through the initiation. Just like the White Plains Wildcats, just like the Lee Flames and our Bucs, our Warrior Cultures demand that a member can't be soft. It's how we define success.

Many of the struggles our players will face are common. But commonality doesn't make it less of a personal struggle. What they're going through may be the first time they've experienced being exposed by their weakness in a certain area. Coaches should help athletes find strength within themselves to overcome these obstacles and stay on the Warrior Path.

Resilience is learned through failure *and* requires mentorship that combines truth with optimism. If we want a team of Warriors, our[11] resilience must be our top priority. We must train it with intentionality. Let's look at some obstacles our players will face and how we can help them overcome.

---

[11] The word "our" is intentional here. Coaches too. More on that in the next chapter.

MISTAKES

A prerequisite for poise is a healthy response to mistakes. This has become a hot topic in coaching communities for a good reason. **Resilience influences outcomes**.

But it isn't as cut and dry as it may seem. Many coaches find themselves at a loss trying to "fix" how their players respond to mistakes. The stance we take on "mistake response" (as Dick Devenzio called it in his book, *Stuff! Good Players Should Know*[12]) goes much deeper than the appropriate action. It cuts straight to the soul of the player. This isn't a behavioral issue. It's a heart issue.

Regarding mistakes, let's consider the three types of athletes we mentioned in the introduction:

Civilians don't handle mistakes well. The mistake triggers a negative emotional reaction, affecting one's level of poise and competitiveness. These emotions torture the person who can't overcome their mistake. "I'm not good enough." "I'm letting the team down." "I'm the unluckiest player in the world."

They are also more likely to pause, drop their head and energy levels. They miss opportunities to hustle down a mistake and make up for it. They sigh, pout, complain, and often curse.[13] This is a person who gets

---

[12] Devenzio, Dick. *Stuff! Good Players Should Know*. Pgc Basketbal; 4th edition, 2014.

[13] Another reason we don't allow our players to use profanity on the floor. Emotionally charged profanity is the adult manifestation of a temper tantrum. It's also a really bad look for teenagers in

stuck in their own head. They lack the emotional strength to move on and learn, often finding themselves in a rut of self-loathing or jealousy.

The Nameless tend to respond well to their own mistakes (even realizing mistakes are necessary for growth). If they struggle with jealousy or self-loathing, they usually have the good sense to keep it to themselves. They're just tough enough to get by with no one noticing their deficiencies. But their weakness is exposed by their response to the mistakes of others. "Others" are teammates, officials, and coaches.

Warriors glean every speck of knowledge from their own mistakes while wasting no time in self-loathing. They don't hesitate after mistakes. They hustle. They realize mistakes are part of the game and wasting a second could mean missing an opportunity.

Warriors also handle the mistakes of "others" with understanding and objective optimism. The "others" feel this reaction. It empowers them to improve. And they definitely appreciate it.

The Warrior has come to grips with one of life's ultimate truisms—some things are out of my control. And one of those things is the past. If something is within the Warrior's control, their positive mistake response owns it and takes action. They work toward solutions, learn from mistakes, and press on. The Warrior has practiced this response for so long, it's a

---

competitive situations. They don't look angry and tough as much they look spoiled and soft.

habit. Their mental process is automated. Instinctual. Unconscious.

The Nameless can be good at positive mistake response. But it requires a conscious decision. And conscious decisions take seconds. In sports, you don't always have seconds to recover. If you hesitate, sometimes you get burned.

Civilians just can't have nice things. They're too busy pouting, to turn it around. They have the uncanny ability to make things that suck exponentially worse. By doing this, Civilians give up control they could have over future outcomes to stay in their state of comfortable misery.

If something isn't within our control, why waste energy whining about it? We have to fight our human nature here. It's easy to complain about the uncontrollable and label them unfair. Well...of course it's unfair. Life is unfair. Read some history.

But Warriors accept what is and fight the urge to become victims. Their pride won't allow them to become victims. **When adversity strikes, a Civilian deflates, a Nameless hesitates, a Warrior activates.**

Elmar Kuli-Zade was the best point guard I've ever coached. He was 5'9 155lb and had a rather large chip on his shoulder, which was understandable since he had only one partial scholarship offer out of high school. But he knew he could play and went to the place that would give him the chance to prove it. But Elmar had a significant advantage. He played harder than anyone he ever played with or against. That was his identity. He was a Warrior.

In January of his Senior year at Lee, we faced rival #2 ranked Southern Polytechnic University. He had become one of the best players in the country, and this top ten battle was the kind of game he lived for. It was a tie game with 12 minutes to play when Elmar knifed through the crowded lane for a highly contested layup. As he reached the peak of his jump, he was knocked off balance, falling face first across the baseline, basically bowling for cheerleaders. He missed the shot, and no foul was called.

A Poly forward grabbed the rebound and threw a swift outlet pass to their point guard, who turned up the floor with one dribble and threw a laser beam up the sideline to their 6'6" All-American swing man. He caught the ball around the hash mark, took two dribbles, and elevated for a thunderous one-handed jam. As he left his feet, Elmar stepped in front of him and took a charge. The whistle blew.
Half the crowd went crazy, the other half held their breath, anticipating the call while wondering if it would be bad form to celebrate their favorite player being dunked on so disrespectfully. The whole crowd erupted as the ref put his hand behind his head to signal a charge call.

I had no idea how Elmar got there in time to make the play. And I am still 99% sure that the official got caught up in the moment because it was an obvious block. It was even more amazing on film. He didn't look at the ref for the foul when he got knocked to the floor, and make no mistake, he got hammered. With no hesitation, he emerged from the pile of cheerleaders and took off in a dead sprint. That's just who he was. When something didn't go his way, he ran straight into the next opportunity to make a play.

He dropped 37 points in that game and willed our team to a double overtime victory. That year, Lee won the conference regular season and tournament championships. Elmar was voted SSAC Player of the Year. That one play tells you all you need to know about why he became a great college basketball player despite his size. He was relentless.

THE MISTAKES OF TEAMMATES

Great players make everyone look better. It's not just their work ethic and confidence rubbing off, although this does happen. It's how the great player plays *with* others. They encourage their teammates through mistakes, empowering them to play to the best of their ability.

When the best player on a team has a habit of reacting positively to the mistakes of their teammates, their teammates play better because they aren't looking over their shoulder. Their game isn't crippled by the fear of disappointing their alpha peer.

Also, great players know the strengths and weaknesses of their teammates and play accordingly, only putting them in positions with a high success rate while still making them feel trusted. In football they call it the *tight-end rule.*

"Lamar, you can't expect Joe to make that catch." Lamar is a great quarterback, so he knows this, and the next time, he fires the ball between the numbers. Even if it goes right through Joe's hands, it hits him in the chest, giving him a chance to corral it in an aesthetically unpleasant but effective way. But move those sticks because Lamar is so good that he knows the exact skill set of his teammate. He butters the bread and makes the sandwich, and all Joe has to do is eat.

If a player thinks they're good, they'll make their teammates better by setting them up for success. They won't live frustrated with their teammate's mistakes. They'll take note. What I see when a player pouts or complains about a teammate's mistakes, is a player who's not good enough to make people better. I see a Nameless.

REFS AND BAD CALLS

Nobody is going to be perfect here, but we have to realize that if we are trying to coach Warriors, we must model the Warrior Way. Remember, teams will take on the personality of their coach. If we had more players that didn't look sideways at officials when calls don't go their way, we'd have more good players. And we'd definitely have more Warriors.[14]

---

[14] Forget about the NBA for a second. Those guys are on such a high level with the smallest margin for error possible that it can't even be considered the same game. We can learn a lot from them, but much of it won't translate to our game. And one thing that would never translate to a high school or college game would be how they treat officials. Imagine what would happen if Draymond Green

We're better if we take more personal responsibility. So that's what we try to do. If a player looks sideways at an official, they're asking me to take them out because that game is too big for them. I tell our players that's the way I see it. And predictably, we don't have many players looking sideways at officials. If a player needs help from the officials, they just aren't very good.[15]

Owning responsibility in basketball looks like this:
I could have taken it to the rim stronger. I will next time.
I could have taken a better angle defensively. I will next time.
I could have jumped to the ball faster. I will next time.

Warriors know that there's almost always something that could have been done better. And we don't give away our game to anyone. We own it. **Whining about calls is admitting to every person in the gym that we aren't good enough.**

It means we need help to succeed. Think of a time you got salty at officials.
Was it a bad shooting night?
Were we the best team on the floor?
Did we *need* those calls?

There are rare exceptions, but most of the time, we want those calls so badly because we need them to compensate for what we are lacking at the moment. So, we have a choice, keep arguing calls... or...

---

carried on and cursed a high school official like he does in the NBA. He wouldn't make it through the first quarter.
[15] This is especially true in high school.

Challenge each other to play/be/get better. In my experience with this approach, our players play better and our staff coaches better. And officials respect that. It's a win on all fronts.

NEGATIVITY AND COMPLAINING

"Resentment and complaint are appropriate neither for oneself nor others."

—Miyamoto Musashi

Our Bucs have a team policy that I presented, and we all agreed upon. NO COMPLAINING. Our players have committed to becoming Warriors. This means they want to solve problems, not complain about them. If a problem is out of their control, they don't waste their breath or time stuck in the stasis of negativity. They move on to the next right thing.

Sometimes, they fail, as do I, but we hold each other to this standard. And because we've already made our decision about complaining, we are more likely to recognize it and self-correct.

All the students who attend our school don't *have* to act like that, but they're certainly encouraged to. But if they're going to play on our basketball team, they do have to act like that. We surround ourselves with Warriors, no exceptions.

This does not mean that a player can't approach anyone on our staff about things that are bothering them. Quite the opposite, to us, confrontation is problem solving. Complaining is problem exacerbating.

Confrontation is honest, eye to eye, heart to heart.
Confrontation is about us.
Complaining is done in the shadows, not forthright.
Complaining is about me.

There's no room for complaining in a Warrior Culture. I will not coach any more players I don't respect. This doesn't mean they have to act like me. Their character or, at the least, their intentions have to be respectable. There is a big difference between bad character and mischief, just like there's a difference between insanity and temporary insanity.

Chronic complaining is a dead giveaway for broken character. And coaches can't help a player who has broken character and doesn't want to repair it. The relationship, as it should be, ends at that point. The player doesn't see the need to change, so they won't. They have to go, or they'll bring good people down with them.

We'd be remiss if we didn't mention how hard this is to do when one of our best players *is* a jerk. Notice I said *is*, not *acts like*. Good kids act like jerks all the time. Heck, so do good adults. We have to call them on it when it happens, and they have to want to be better and desire change. And most of the time they will.

But If they don't want to change, their squirrelly behavior becomes *is-ness*. And when someone *is* a jerk who has no remorse in their heart, they aren't changing.

I've never, not once, ever talked to a coach who regretted kicking off a talented player who *was* a jerk. I've talked to hundreds who wished they had, or had sooner, sent their jerk packing. We know this as addition by subtraction. Even if it's one of our best players who *is* soft and selfish, we have to do ourselves a favor and cut the cord. Our lives will be better and our teams will probably thank us for it. They get sick of selfish behavior, too.

Conversational complaining is another funny thing when we think about it. Imagine being at a party with friends when someone complains about their job. Now think of how much you thought about those complaints that next week. Probably zero times. Don't care now and didn't care then. It was a complete waste of conversation time. That's the thing about complaining, nobody cares.

I wish I learned that earlier in my life. It's embarrassing to think I have missed a truth so obvious, that while complaining about petty this or inconvenient that, I was dumping on the sensibilities of anyone who enjoys pleasant conversation. And offending any Warrior with my display of first-world entitlement and softness.

If complaining becomes part of one's personality, they will become an insufferable bore quickly. "Hey, [insert name], can you complain more to me today? I really enjoyed being a sounding board for your venting last time," said nobody ever. I can't remember ever being excited to see a chronically negative person.

Chronically negative people become self-fulfilling prophecies. Their existence sucks. Literally, it sucks the life out of anyone unfortunate enough to cross their path. But in my short time on this earth I've learned (often by doing the opposite) that I don't have to worry about them, nor should I. There's a reason under-achievers hang out with other under-achievers—they have common ground. They get each other.

I have no beef over them mobbing up and gossiping about how they're all getting screwed over. That keeps them, their toxic philosophies, conspiracy theories, and overall contagious negativity out of my face. And away from our team. We find the same pack mentality in high achievers. They usually hang out with other high achievers. Life's too short to waste it on toxic people, so we want to be sure they stay out of our space.

One more thing nobody cares about—excuses. In February 2020, Tyson Fury battered Deontay Wilder in their second fight. It was such a one-sided romp that Wilder's trainer threw in the towel, stopping the fight in the 7th round. Wilder had a plethora of excuses for his poor performance and the beating he took. But the excuse that really stood out was his claim that his walkout costume was too heavy, and his legs were tired as a result. Come on, man.

The internet didn't care. Deontay Wilder got roasted for his excuse. Nobody wanted to hear that.

THE UNDERDOG COMEBACK STORY. WE LOVE IT

In 1779, as America was fighting to gain independence from the British, Warrior Culture left its fingerprints all over the action.

The hopeful Americans were working with a scrapped together force using donations of men and supplies from other countries supporting their cause. Not to mention adjusting to a mightier force on the fly. Perhaps, the best example of this was the fledgling American Navy and the Battle of Flamborough Head.

Captain John Paul Jones made his name during the American Revolution although the way that name should go down in history is up for debate. To many, he was the "Father of the American Navy", while others say he was nothing more than a pirate looking to take advantage of open waters at wartime. Either way, he wasn't a guy you wanted to tangle with on the high seas. Like many wartime stories, sometimes lore gets mixed with facts and what remains is legend.
One thing history agrees on is that on September 23, 1779, Jones captained a merchant ship converted into a 42-gun wartime vessel named the *Bonhomme Richard* and led a fleet of 4 French and American ships in the North Sea. Unexpectedly, they encountered two English heavy hitters coming in from the open ocean, and the fight began.

Tactically, Jones was known as a wildcard who relied on instincts and unorthodox strategies. Without the benefit of a formal Naval education, he clashed with other captains in his fleet and even occasionally dealt with insubordination from his own crew.

As the ships engaged, Jones, expecting support from his fleet, found himself pursued by the far superior English ship, the *Serapis*. Unfortunately for Jones and his ship, he didn't see help on the way. They were outmatched and outgunned, and as the firing ensued, he had a decision to make.

Standard fighting, which would be a losing proposition.
or...
Break script and take a chance on something that was so crazy it might work.

Jones was a Warrior, and he did what Warriors do. Knowing that any battle dictated by the two ships squaring off would cause sure defeat, Jones ordered the *Bonhomme Richard* onto a direct collision course with the *Serapis*. His bold plan was to make contact between the ships, board the enemy boat, and take this fight hand to hand.

On first contact, Captain Richard Pearson of the *Serapis* mockingly shouted to his American foe, "Has your ship struck?"
To which Jones responded, "I have not yet begun to fight!"
Then things got wild.

He ordered his ship to keep ramming the *Serapis* while they took fire from British cannons. Waves crashing and splinters flying, they finally succeeded in ramming the vessel so hard that the two masts became entangled, allowing his crew time to board the ship. For hours, the two ships blasted each other from close range with heavy artillery amid the chaos of hand to hand combat. In my imagination, I see sailors jumping from deck to deck, swinging from ropes, and having the time of their lives.

The *Bonhomme Richard* began taking on water, and it looked like surrender was the only option for Jones and his men. But Jones knew that because the boats were tied together, if his ship went down, it would take the *Serapis* with her. Faced with certain defeat, he refused to give up and urged his men to fight on.

Finally, the rest of the American fleet showed up, and the tables had turned. Suddenly outnumbered, the British relented, surrendering the *Serapis* to John Paul Jones in one of the most bewildering upsets in the history of the American Navy.

Under a white flag, Captain Pearson had to board the remains of the *Bonhomme Richard* and ceremoniously hand over his saber to the American captain, cementing John Paul Jones as a name history would remember.

Everybody loves a good underdog story, especially if there's a comeback involved. Hollywood can crank out the same script over and over and we'll pay to see it. And we'll like it.

Maybe it has something to do with being able to relate and root for characters who remind us of ourselves. It's easy to get emotionally sucked into those plot twists and be swept away when the game-winning shot goes in.

But here's the thing, at some point, something had to go wrong in order for those situations to occur. It's impossible to come back if you never got down in the first place, and there's no such thing as an underdog that starts out as the favorite.

Every story worth telling casts adversity as a central character.

What if I told you I wrote a screenplay—Boy or girl gets a job. Makes a good living. Gets along with everyone. Gets married. Has family. Nothing goes wrong. Everyone's happy and eats popcorn watching movies about underdog comeback stories. For the life of me, I can't figure out why Netflix won't pick up this script. Oh, yeah… It's boring.

Adversity is coming. Every season, most weeks, and sometimes it seems like every day. In our best seasons and our worst seasons, it will be there. There's an old coaching adage that says our teams will go through at least three major crises every year, and our success will be determined by how we handle them.

Warrior Culture uses challenging events to become a stronger, better team. Civilian teams splinter and crack under the weight of pressure.

We don't always have control over when things get rough. It would be convenient if we could schedule our best player's nagging hip flexor issue for Christmas break, or if we could ask the faculty to not schedule any big tests on game day.

The correct response to adversity refuses to let any member become a victim. Every obstacle is an opportunity.

THE TRUTH AND OUR STORIES

"Truth is not what you want it to be. It is what it is, and you must bend to its power or live a lie."

—Miyamoto Musashi

Most have heard Jack Canfield's success formula,
Event + Response = Outcome[16]
It's become a popular, useful catch phrase circulating the sports world, rehashed on Twitter the past few years to the point where you'd be hard pressed to miss it. It puts a great vantage point on owning our decision-making and rejecting the victim mindset. It's easy to remember and fits great on a bumper sticker, but life is rarely that simple.

Much like the story of John Paul Jones, the truth of an event is often subject to the person telling the story. In 1779, whether you thought Jones was a pirate or Naval hero probably depended on what side of the ocean you called home.

---

[16] Canfield, J. *The Success Principles – How to Get from Where You Are to Where You Want to Be.* William Morrow Paperbacks; 10th Anniversary Edition, 2015

A missing piece to the E+R=O formula is the *truth*. Events must be observed through a lens of objectivity. Objective truth is vital to decision-making. But, for teenagers, it's hard to come by without help from an expert that isn't family or a friend.

As coaches, we do our players a great disservice if we sugarcoat the truth or avoid the hard conversations. Sure, we should deliver truth with grace, but we have a responsibility to deliver it.

In many cases, a coach is the only adult in a young person's life that will tell them the truth about their ability, performance, and attitude. We can't expect them to accept it easily. But we can be committed to truth, and that commitment will eventually build trust.

When an event is competitive, like sports, objectivity often goes out the window. Correct responses require true stories. And our sports stories can be swayed by emotion and bias. This is why truth can be so hard to discern in competition.

> *"In strategy, it is important to see distant things as if they were close and to take a distanced view of close things."*
> —Miyamoto Musashi

Our feelings can influence the stories we tell ourselves about our lives. Feelings are valid, but they must be balanced to be grounded in reality. In fiction, a strictly subjective narrator is exciting but unreliable.

However, a reliable objective narrator is often void of personality. They're boring.
Because we love excitement, we rarely ignore our feelings (our story), but often ignore objective truth.

Warriors view their feelings under the microscope of objective truth. This keeps them from beating up themselves and allows them to assess and self-correct when necessary.

Look at Jones' situation:
Event: He was sailing in the North Sea counting on his teammates to back him up when he was engaged by a superior ship.
Warrior Mindset: The first thing to note is that he wasted zero time bemoaning the fact that he was battling alone when he should have had back up. Warriors don't make excuses when they can't be adjusted, they embrace the tough.

Truth: He took an objective look at the reality of the situation. He knew that a straight up Naval duel in the middle of the sea was a surefire way to be capsized. And although there is a lot of honor for the Captain going down with the ship, isn't there more to be said for accepting the objective truth of the situation and adjusting to the circumstances based on those facts?

Response: A "so crazy it just might work" collision to bring the fight to them.

Outcome: John Paul Jones and his crew won the day, and "I have not yet begun to fight" goes down as a great moment in trash talk history.

In any professional field, the key to making good decisions is good information. Regarding sports, everyone we know has opinions, and they won't all be accurate. When it comes to our events, we need people around us that will tell us the truth in the interest of our improvement.

All we can do is the best we can with our resources and abilities. Maximum effort guided by the truth tips the scales to our advantage, giving us our best chance to win.

Just because John Paul Jones responded like a Warrior, his victory wasn't guaranteed. But his response gave him a chance. He did all he could do, like a Warrior would, but he also caught a lucky break to secure the win. **Luck often smiles on people who are doing the best they can with what they have.**

Warriors don't make excuses for their situations. They accept them and move quickly and decisively. And on a long enough timeline, this approach becomes a habit. That's worth repeating because people often get deflated when their work doesn't produce their desired outcome. And this deflation can inhibit their Warrior mentality later.

Outcomes Are Never Guaranteed

We have to embrace the fact that no matter what our response, outcomes are never guaranteed. Knowing this, Warriors don't act merely for outcomes. They act with intelligence, courage, and resilience because it's who they want to be.

The reality of unknown outcomes, even though it can be unnerving at first glance, isn't so bad. It's what makes life brimming with possibilities and inspiring stories of strength. Everyone loves the comeback story. And even more, the *rising from the ashes* story.

Expectations *will* be shattered. Sometimes, even when we've done everything right. It's just life as the Warrior knows it to be. Civilians and many of the Nameless haven't accepted this. They work as if the result will be inevitably positive. As if their work is a transaction that will always end with their desired outcome.

And when inevitable suffering occurs, those who are not living the Warrior Way will most likely become disenfranchised, depressed, and crushed under the weight of their disappointment. Their problems lie not in the outcome itself, but in a weak worldview built on a shaky foundation and misplaced desires.

When tangible, measurable outcomes (wins, losses, championships, awards, etc.) are the only desires, the will of an aspiring Warrior can break down when those possibilities are vaporized. This is what it really means to quit.

When the desired outcome is pride, self-respect, and an unflinching pursuit of the Warrior Way, an athlete measures an outcome in terms of their soul. They will never give up. They will fight to the bitter end, proving their worth to not only themselves, but every person within eyeshot of their performance.

They face inevitable adversity with predetermined[17] actions instead of emotional[18] reactions. They attack problems with flexibility. Warriors don't do it for outcomes. They fight because it's who they are, and the outcomes (good and bad) take care of themselves without taking anything away the experience of the fight itself.

The Warrior decides to be a Warrior before the adversity arrives. And before the ball is ever tipped.

---

[17] Hustle, confident body language, encouragement of teammates.
[18] Pout, tantrum, give up.

Chapter 4

The Hard Stuff for Coaches

"You have to bring up your innermost darkness to the surface in order to see the light of day and change."

—Peter Rollins

High school coaching is not an easy job. The competition is fierce. The hours are brutal. The hats we wear are many. There are so many problems to solve, young people to coach up, and complicated relationships and emotions to navigate. But man, it can be so fulfilling. Until it's not.

Think back to a time when you got a new job. The administration believed in you enough to hire you. Your voice was fresh and inspiring to the players. The excitement of each day trumped the petty problems you faced. You were trusted, loved, and listened to. You were having fun.

Then, the petty problems added up. Your voice, once so alive and vibrant, became like an overplayed pop song on the radio. The people around you became difficult to work with, selfish, and even skeptical or pessimistic.

And after the first or second or third particularly challenging season filled with problems coming at you from angles you didn't even realize were there, you became like the people who made your job hard. Without even knowing how it went bad so fast, you dusted off your resume and looked for greener pastures.

We do this all the time. And many coaches accept this merry-go-round as just *part of the job*. Some of us have spent entire careers on this ride. This might be hard to hear, but I'm going to say it anyway because I have to tell it to myself... A lot...
Maybe my petty problem is me.

This pill is hard to swallow. But if we acknowledge the possibility and swallow it, it will change us. Almost like a vaccine. Not that we'll be healed from getting down, staggered, or upset by the difficulties we'll face. But we'll be able to self-correct and gather the strength to get up, find a way, and do the best we can.

If we can't do that, we have to realize we are the problem. And we're a fraud for still teaching the Warrior Way. How can we ask our players to be Warriors if we are not?
Warrior Culture demands we control what we can control. And let go of what we can't.

ADMINISTRATION PROBLEMS

Do we have control?

Most of the time the answer is no. So perhaps, we should avoid complaining about our administration. Not only are we demotivating ourselves, but it distracts us from the job at hand and the problems we could solve.

Complaining to or about our administrations may get us what we want for a few seasons, but that song and dance gets old. In time, administrators grow weary of high-maintenance coaches. If our habit is complaining our way to the administrative support we desire, we'll always be a season or two from hearing these words...

"We've decided to take the program in a different direction."

And honestly, can we blame the administrations? What if someone complained and tried to strong-arm their way into getting you to make coaching decisions that were in their personal best interest?

Oh yeah, that happens all the time. They are called entitled parents. Well, how do we feel about them?

When we get outside ourselves to the point we can see things through the eyes of others, we become better people. It's easy to say, but takes intentionality to live out.

So, what if we truly believe that some things need to change? How can our voice be heard without coming off as a complainer to our administration? [19]

We should just do our jobs as well as we can. And if we want more control, we have to prove our value to the institution. Volunteer for minor jobs outside of our sport. Meet everyone. Make them feel important.

If we want a say in administrative decisions, we should make ourselves so valuable to the school that the administration considers asking for our input.

If nobody is asking, I'd suggest stop giving unsolicited advice. Unsolicited advice rarely works in real life, what makes us think it would be an effective strategy with our administration?
The simple fact is... it's not.

FEEDER SCHOOLS, NUMBERS, AND GYM SPACE

I hear many coaches complaining about their feeder school problems and lack of numbers. I understand it is frustrating to not have the resources others do, but there are many strategies we can use to counteract this disadvantage. To name a few—Run great summer camps. Get involved with AAU. Run group training sessions. And most important of all, win. If you win, players will come.

---

[19] When it comes to our school administration we must always operate under the assumption that they are doing the best they can. I had to learn that lesson the hard way.

The gym space complaint just doesn't jive with me. It's inconvenient. But there is so much we can do to flip this script and become a better coach *because* of the gym-space challenge, not in spite of it. We are forced into the *opportunity* to make our practices more efficient.

Turning challenges, inconveniences, and difficult situations into opportunities is a pillar of Warrior Culture.

Also, we could call every gym in the city to see if we can get some free floor time. We could practice in the mornings before school. There are so many ways we could attack this problem. Let's call complaining about this what it is—A Civilian response. The Warrior would find a way.

Refs

We're all competitive. I get that. But what do we accomplish when we complain about calls we can't change?

For me, I lose time coaching. A play could be drawn up, or a player taught, or someone encouraged. Not to mention the action that I need to be watching. Yet, here I am. Whining about a call to no avail. No advantage being gained. Most of the time I'm contesting a call, I'm missing things that would make me better at my job. And even though there are times we can gain an advantage by bringing something to a ref's attention, contesting past calls is almost always a futile endeavor.

We might get, "I mighta missed that one, coach." That's the best we can hope for. **The best response we can hope for still won't change the call.** Calls never get changed in basketball, and rarely in football.[20] Our time is better spent adapting, adjusting, and coaching our players.

I'm reminding myself here, too. This one is tough because we're competitive and sports are emotional. And the more competitive we are, the more can get caught up in the emotion of the moment. We can't remind ourselves enough. And we can't let competing handicap our coaching.

The Warrior Coach has a higher, more noble calling than working the referees to get a few 50/50 calls. And that's pouring our soul into coaching our players. There's only so much in the tank. Let's use our passion for those in our locker room.

PLAYER MOTIVATION (OR LACK THEREOF)

We have to get over our personal passion for our sport and get real here. Young athletes don't understand how much work it takes to achieve competitive greatness. And while we need to help them understand, we also must accept that many will have

---

[20] Clemson vs. Ohio State in the 2020 college football playoff (I'm still not over it). Fans reserve the right to be Civilians. It's a right that comes with paying to go to games. Coaches get paid. We forfeit the right to be Civilians.

no desire to achieve competitive greatness in a sport that they won't play much by the time they can legally enjoy a cold beer.

Fact—The vast majority of high school players are recreational. They love to compete, love their teammates, love the atmosphere, and love being on the team. They *like* the sport.

But for some odd reason, we're disappointed that they don't love it like we do. Well, of course they don't. We are coaches. We have made a conscious decision to dedicate our professional lives to this sport. Our athletes are going to grow up to be business professionals, musicians, teachers, salespeople, chefs, vets, doctors, internet personalities, and anything else you can imagine. Why would they be as passionate about it as we are?

We can't control how much they love basketball. And if we could, would berating our young people for not caring enough be the best way to solve this problem? Doubtful.

And if all our players had the passion of a coach, more of them would choose to coach as a profession. If that happened, would there be enough coaching jobs out there for them?

The easy answer is no because the job market is already saturated as it is.

Maybe they love being a Warrior and playing in a Warrior Culture, but don't care to acquire the skills to make themselves collegiate in the sport we coach. Is that so bad? Is there a place for these players in our Warrior Culture? Of course, there is.

Some of my favorite players I've ever coached didn't care enough to put in the work to become collegiate. But during our season, they'd play their hearts out. Unselfishly. Throwing a drenched jersey in the hamper after every practice. Bleeding on the floor. Battling every game. Training the Warrior within as a Nameless basketball player on a great team.

And later in life, this Warrior will do great things. And I'd like to think they'd look back on a sport they played for fun with fondness and gratitude. For the team of Warrior brothers or sisters they got to spend each day with. For the coach who cared about the person they were becoming more than the player they were. For the program that was bigger than any individual. For the things they learned about themselves. And the Warrior Spirit they worked so hard to unleash.

I'd like to think their education was enhanced by playing our sport. And we all, coaches and teammates, played a part in their development. But this is unlikely to happen if our recreational players can't enjoy the game for what it is—a game. An intense, competitive, **fun** practice for the rest of their lives.

Maybe we should do our best to maximize their enjoyment of our sport. **We will get more out of our players if we accept who they are instead of being bitter about who they are not.**

HARD COACHING

"My father gave me the greatest gift anyone could give another person. He believed in me."

—Jim Valvano

Let that settle for a minute. Coaching is people + strategy. In our quest for optimal competitive strategy, we often undervalue the personality needs of the people necessary to make our strategy successful.

If success is the goal, criticism will always be part of the equation, BUT... it can't be all criticism and correction. With many young athletes, it can't even be 50/50 criticism and affirmation. They need a ton of encouragement. They need to believe that the person, whose professional opinion they respect[21], believes in them before they can stop beating themselves up over what we think are standard critiques.

There's a fascinating power dynamic between coaches and players. Boundaries are certainly necessary because the last thing we want is to become *one of the guys*. That would suppress the effectiveness of our voice and can undermine our respectability for the immature athletes.[22]

---

[21] It is the leader's job to be respectable. Respect is earned by the combination of a leader's character and strategic skill and people skills. Lacking in any of these areas will limit respectability.

[22] Expectation management—They are in high school so there will be a significant amount of immaturity.

The personal walls between coaches and players need to be broken down for optimal growth to occur. Unpopular opinion incoming—A coach's likeability may be the most underrated aspect of high school coaching. But hear me out.

Old school coaching philosophy says the coach doesn't have to be liked. But today, teenagers tend to not listen to people they don't like.

We could take that argument further and find that maybe it isn't only teenagers who are like that. If my worst enemy gave me constructive criticism, I would likely think it was stupid or hurtful. If a person I like and have utmost respect for gave me the exact same advice, I'd probably consider it brilliant and helpful. That's human nature.

We should consider the possibility that this old school coaching philosophy hasn't aged well. It may be flawed when it comes to a basic understanding of people. It may or may not have always been wrong. But it's most certainly wrong when coaching this generation of teenager.

Most humans, whether or not they admit it, want to be liked. Our need for social acceptance is in the fabric of our DNA. Judging by witnessing the social media habits of today's young people, I'd venture to guess that being liked is "kind of a big deal" to them.

"I don't care if you like me or not" is the coaching approach that we're all familiar with. But what if it's fundamentally flawed? What if kids haven't changed? What if the problem is that we forgot what it was like to be a kid?

It's convenient to blame the generation gap for our inability to connect with kids. Without purposeful mindfulness to ponder all aspects of a disconnect, it's easy to fall back on the most convenient explanations. The one that absolves me, the coach, of guilt.

What if a grossly underestimated value of leadership *is* being liked by those who follow? I know that *liked* is not a word coaches are comfortable with, but growth comes from places of discomfort.

We need to consider what is important to people in order to lead them. If it's a big deal to kids to be liked, then it's also important that they like their leader. Just like the Warrior wouldn't want to go to battle with one they don't respect. Because, To the Warrior, being respected is "kind of a big deal."

I sense that a mature adult might say, "But the kids shouldn't care so much about being liked." Again, convenient. Yeah, maybe this emotionally mature adult could say that. But high school players aren't emotionally mature adults. They're kids.

Our ability to inspire is enhanced by our charisma. And maybe we *need* our players to like us more than we once thought. This doesn't mean, as my grandad would say, "the inmates will run the asylum." Being liked isn't compromising when we see unacceptable behavior. Quite the opposite—It's proactive, giving the best chance to inspire the behaviors we want to see.

Kids want structure. They also want to please, unless they think their coach is a jerk who doesn't care about them as a person. When we like them,[23] and our actions show we care about them as people rather than just players, we may find ourselves coaching a team of inspired Warriors that would run through that proverbial "brick wall" for us.

Circling back to a concept that can't be emphasized enough, the more we love them, the more we can coach/criticize them. They will be more open to our truth. Loving our players is knowing them, liking them, and believing in them. The more we *know* their personality because we've taken the time to learn about them, the more receptive they'll be when we have to coach them hard.

There are many times when we feel the urge to coach them hard, but a rough stretch of losses and the collective temperature of our team calls for a prescription of positive reinforcement rather than negative feedback. In these moments, we must get over the frustration we feel the urge to release, and instead, be the steady voice of courage our players need to hear.

---

[23] And this is impossible to fake. Kids usually have a better "fake" detector than adults. My guess about the reason for this is adults have been faking for so much longer that they've become desensitized to fakeness. They've developed a tolerance that's led to a high level of immunity. Ignorance is bliss.

Sometimes, love means showing restraint and knowing when to avoid nagging. Young people hate feeling constantly piled on. Not just young people. All people. If we aren't careful and balanced in our approach, we might think we're coaching while they think we're a bully. Intent is irrelevant when a person feels attacked. A positive, likeable person is the leader young people want to fight their best for. Maybe not *for—alongside.*

Chapter 5

Parents

It sounds like a great job, but how are the parents? One of the first thoughts when we consider the drawbacks of being a high school coach is parents. There is a very distinct feeling when you get an email at 11:30 pm from a familiar last name with the subject heading "Meeting Tomorrow?" There's an even worse feeling if that request comes in person, immediately after a game.

Eventually, we will have issues with a parent. It's coming. A season without a single parent complaining or calling for a meeting is not a reflection of a program without parent issues, it probably just means those issues are manifesting in other ways.

Basketball is emotionally charged and played on a public display. Our athletes physically decide the outcome. Our coaching decisions can affect the outcome, too. We have to understand that most of our parents have the same (if not a higher) level of emotion but no control over outcomes, and that's hard.

Sports parents experience a wide spectrum of emotions from natural protection instincts (physical play, safety, bad calls) to societal perception (desire for a college scholarship opportunity) and even personal identity issues (parents that force their own worth on the athletic performance of their kid). And so many more.

Each parent will have a unique mix of issues they bring to the table and their own way of revealing them. Sometimes they'll be direct. But more often their issues are manifested passive-aggressively behind closed doors in interactions with their kid.

Parent issues don't change the job we have to do, but it *does* make it harder. Unfortunately, we have to work tactfully against competing voices in the ears of our players. But before we hold that against our players, we have to remember, none of them chose their parents.

Their parents rocked them to sleep as babies, kissed their first boo-boo, taught them how to fish or ride a bike, and bought them Christmas presents every year. We've done none of those things. We can't compete with that.

There will be times when we will hear the obnoxious parent in the top row screaming, "C'MON COACH! WHAT ARE WE DOING?" We know they are embarrassing themselves, but we also can feel every eyeball that followed the path of those words from the top of the bleachers to the front of our bench.

On that island, we may even think, *How can a grown adult act that way in public?* But that's because when the unwelcome spotlight is shining on us, we have a selective memory about the irrationality of passion.

In January 2020, our Bucs were undefeated in District play. Since we had moved to a tougher league in 2016, we hadn't won a District regular season or tournament championship. The year before we finished second in the regular season standings. This was the year we would get over the hump. We had the ability and had done the work. We could taste it.

It was a Friday home game, and the gym was packed. We were hosting a worthy opponent. Every game we'd played against them since I'd been coaching at Boyd had been an all-out war. They were as well-coached as any team in the city and every bit as tough as us. Both teams were known for in-your-face, lockdown half-court defense. We were ranked #1 and #2 in the state (all classifications) in scoring defense (points allowed per-game). And since we're all about honesty in Warrior Culture, we have to admit that neither team was an offensive juggernaut.

Both coaches knew it was going to be a low scoring grind every time we played. Everyone in the gym, even the officials, knew how tense these games would get because the margin for error was so small and the stakes were so high.

The atmosphere was electric from the tip. The game went back-and-forth, and the student bodies followed suit with creative back-and-forth trash talk chants. Midway through the second quarter, our leading scorer drove the lane. A defender stepped in to draw a charge. Our guy change direction with a pro hop. There was contact, most of which was the ball hitting the defender. The defender turned his shoulder and fell sideways in a different direction than our guy was heading. Of course, this is the way I saw it.

The whistle blew, the ball went in, and I pumped my fist fully expecting the official to signal a block and punch in the bucket. But with a point toward the other basket, the hand went behind the head, signaling the charge. The official saw it different. That hurt because in these high-intensity, low-scoring grinders, a 3 the old-fashioned way felt like a 7.

"Do you think he was set?" I asked when she took her position in front of my bench during the next play.
"He had a legal guarding position," she replied.
I responded complete with hand motions[24], "Really? Because it looked to me like he turned sideways, then fell sideways."

It was loud in there, and our voices were naturally raised. Which surely sounded to the other like we were yelling even though neither of us intentionally started the conversation that way. Emotionally charged environment problems.

"He stepped in FRONT. YOU'RE GUY ran over him!" she said.
"He turned SIDEWAYS. AND FELL THE WRONG WAY!"
"IT WAS A LEGAL GUARDING POSITION!" She yelled while a whistle across the floor stopped the action.
"HOW CAN HE... (a bunch of stuff I can't remember)!" I yelled at her while she ran backwards down the floor. The volume of my voice raised with every syllable while she got further away. My hand motions ran wilder. My dad, who was on our staff, stood and grabbed my arm, trying to calm me down. Wasn't

---

[24] Bonus tip—Officials hate hand and body gestures. I'm now aware that they have never worked to my benefit. They are simply not-so-subtle ways of grandstanding the ref to make them look bad. Even if it's not what we are meaning to do, it doesn't matter. Remember, it's not what we say, it's what is heard. I used to think I was smart when I did this, now I realize that while I thought I communicating effectively, they had stopped listening because all they cared about was getting me to stop making a scene. And that's fair. Nobody wants to be grandstanded.

happening. I ripped my arm out of his grasp. And continued to make a scene.

And of course, I got popped with a T. It happens. But my word, this could've been avoided if I didn't let my emotions get the best of me.

I led with a rhetorical question. *I* didn't really want a reply. What *I* wanted was for everyone in the gym to see the ref had messed up. *I* just had to point that out. *I* wanted to embarrass her a little. *I* wanted everyone to think *I* was taking up for my guys. There were a lot of *I*'s sounding off in my head.

And *I* don't like being yelled at, especially in public. Wow. When the shoe is on the other foot, *I* don't like it.
Maybe I should keep that in mind when I consider publicly yelling at our players or refs.
Maybe I shouldn't be surprised by the emotional reactions I incite when I lose my cool.

Our state association has a seatbelt rule for coaches who get a technical during a game. So, I was glued to the bench, unable to help our team because I couldn't communicate effectively in such a loud atmosphere. We lost that night, and my loss of control played a role in our defeat. Our opponent went on to win the regular season District Championship because both teams had only one loss, and they held the tie-breaker.

After the game. I was embarrassed at the tantrum I'd thrown. Worse, everything I'd demonstrated to our team and fans was contrary to our Warrior Culture. There was no "GOOD" in my vocabulary in that moment, and our team paid the price. Live and learn.

What is it about love that turns rational human beings into maniacs? When emotion, passion, and deep desire collide, we often get an extreme view of ourselves. That can be the best *and* worst thing about sports.

Now take our love for sports and magnify it by 10,000, maybe 10 million, and we might be close to how emotional parents are about their children. Yet somehow, we expect their emotional passion to be tempered by objectivity at all times. And if it's not—they're wrong, out of control, insane parents.

The reality might be—They just love their kid.
A sports parent acting out usually isn't a malicious act, but a weak moment where objective truth has been blocked by the strongest love on the planet—A parent's love for their child.

If this is the case, shouldn't we take their feedback less personally? Could we feel less attacked when they question us? It's also possible that their absurd (to us) actions aren't even about us. Maybe they had a rough day at work. With this in mind, it should be easier to keep our cool even in the most incendiary of parent interactions.

The coach/parent dynamic presents another interesting predicament. If we don't have them in the stands, supporting their kids, the team, and us, it can be hard to maximize the growth of our players. And whether we like it or not, it adds more responsibility to our already demanding work hours. Car rides, team meals, volunteer sign-ups, communication. Involved parents help so much with this stuff, which gives us more time for our families and film.

However, if they are going to be involved, eventually we will run into conflict. The quicker we can get over the offensive nature of being questioned and work to get everyone on the same page, the better off we'll all be.

PRESEASON PARENT MEETINGS

These meetings are important for the tone for the year. In our experience, the most beneficial aspect of a preseason in-person parent meeting is it's our chance to humanize ourselves and establish the rules for conflict when it arises.[25]

But we aren't going to insult anyone's intelligence or waste time talking about the ins and outs of the information we should bring to these meetings. Most coaches have this stuff down to a science. What we do want to address is the personal aspect of group and individual parent interactions.

One of the best things I've heard (and immediately stole) from another coach is telling parents, "At some point this year you'll feel like your athlete should have played more, scored more, had a bigger role, or whatever. And you might be right. But I can promise you, I want what's best for this team and your son, and I'm just doing my best."

In our preseason parent meetings, we must be sure there's no doubt we care about their kids. And we have to keep it real. Oh, yeah... and tell a few jokes. It helps if the parents like us, too.

---

[25] "Please email to set up a meeting rather than approach me after the game. I've gotten into post-game fights before. I don't trust myself."
This is a direct quote from one of my parent meetings. Everyone laughed and figured I was probably joking.
I said, "I'm not even joking." They laughed harder assuming it was the next level of an already funny joke. But I guess there was enough uncertainty because none of those parents ever approached me after a game. They never even sent me an email. Fun year.

RECRUITING BELIEVERS IN WARRIOR CULTURE

In our best years, we can't make everyone happy. Even knowing that, there's a sinking feeling when we get that text or email from a parent asking for a meeting. Our natural reaction is to become defensive. We think of times we may have been too hard on their kid or given them less than they deserved. Early in my career, I'd try to think of the talking points that would prove me right. I didn't walk in to these meetings to listen and respond with truth and empathy. I walked in to lecture. Funny thing is—I hate when people do that to me.

There's a big difference between working toward validation and working toward solutions. It's taken great parents to show me that.

A coaching buddy of mine told me a story of a parent who asked for a meeting with him. His son was a Sophomore and had been underperforming. The player's father was ex-military and a big guy who could've been intimidating if he wanted to be. My friend was expecting him to come in hot.

But he came in, with his son behind him, grateful. He told him his son had college dreams and wanted to transfer because he wasn't getting enough minutes. Then he told my friend that wasn't happening, and he asked what his son needed to do to get better and make his college dream more realistic.

My friend was floored, and for the next 30 minutes, they talked about the expectations of the program, the expectations of his son, what he was doing well, where he was coming up short, and what he needed to do to improve and get more playing time. Then they talked about a development plan that would help his son move closer toward making his dream a reality. And what that would look like on a daily basis. They shook hands, and the father said, "If he wants to do it, he will. You won't hear excuses from us."

Over the next few years, that player improved at a phenomenal rate. He became an All-State performer and earned a college scholarship. If only all of our parents had a Warrior Spirit that accepted the objective truth that needs to be injected into the stories our children tell themselves.

I had a meeting with a parent that didn't turn out as well. It was my first year coaching in Memphis, Tennessee. That city is known for producing Division 1 talent, and this kid was as athletic as any I've ever coached. It was a *let me tell you about Little Johnny* meeting.[26]

He told me all about Johnny. How great of an athlete he was. How he had D1 offers in another sport but loved basketball. And how he really was a good kid who was misunderstood. And how I needed to help him stay on his grades. And how all the misdeeds of his past had a reasonable explanation.

---

[26] His name wasn't Johnny, and he wasn't little. But you get the idea.

Each *how* raised more concerns. Truthfully, I didn't know Little Johnny from Adam. When I first met him, he seemed like a good kid. But his Dad sure thought his baby boy had hung the moon.

Little Johnny and I got along fine for most of the season. But as our schedule got tougher, he wasn't performing to the standard he was used to. This kid was a great competitor but struggled to have a healthy mindset about not playing well. It seemed he wanted to be a Warrior. But he was having a hard time walking the Path because he was used to being the star of the show at school and, I imagine based on our earlier parent meeting, at home too.

Predictably, he kept playing worse. Other players stepped up. His role diminished, and his frustration started getting the best of him. He forced tough shots, pass faked at wide open teammates, and even yelled at our younger players for physical mistakes.

After it came to a head during one of the biggest games of the season, we met in my office the next day. I told him his behavior was unacceptable in our program, and that it would be in everyone's best interest if he decided to hang it up and focus on the sport he would play in college the next year. I didn't necessarily give him a choice, but I fully expected him to ask for another chance. I guess I was hoping he wanted to change. But he never asked for another chance and didn't defend himself. He actually looked relieved.

But his dad sure wasn't happy. Sometimes, parents and their kids are on totally different wavelengths. He came storming into practice that day to give me a piece of his mind. I let my assistants run the drills and walked over to hear him out. He had a lot to say. None of it nice. And that was fine. He loved his boy. But his emotions couldn't change the decision we all knew was right. He said his piece and left, and I never heard from him again.

If we keep our cool in interactions like this one, angry parents will often just say what they need to say and leave. It'll be over. Sometimes, they just want to get it all out. Sometimes, they just want to be heard. Sometimes, their lashing out isn't even about us. It's carryover rage from an entirely different part of their lives. Sports are an easy target for misplaced anger, and coaches are the easiest target in sports. Well, us and officials. We have to accept this and know that it's probably best to keep calm.

But it's not always easy to keep cool. It's definitely a best practice, but we live in the real world and sometimes people decide to up the ante on irrationality. The last thing we want to be is a pushover. Coaches aren't wired that way. And we don't want to enable logic and language that will be harmful to our players and the program. This means we have an obligation to speak our truths even if it might cause an emotional reaction.

I had one such explosive parent meeting with the father of one of the most talented high school players I've coached. The kid was a freshman and started from day 1. I don't even remember what happened, but early in the season, his dad got salty and wanted to meet. I obliged.

We sat in our athletic director's office. He wanted to talk strategy and what he thought we should be doing. I didn't appreciate that because I'd already made the guidelines clear that I wouldn't be talking strategy or playing time in parent meetings. But whatever, it happens.

It was a tough situation, because I liked this parent. He had coached AAU basketball and trained many underprivileged kids in the community. But even with the good heart and knowledge he had, he didn't have an objective opinion about our approach to strategy. And I understood that, but he was strong-willed and idealistic, two attributes that I can't deny have been very present in my personality at times.

Every point and counterpoint amplified tension. Our athletic director sat in his chair, attempting to referee the meeting, but our visions for our team clashed. I wasn't changing, nor did I feel it would be best to do so. After about 15 minutes of neither of us backing down an inch, our AD advised a break to cool off. We both agreed. He went for a walk outside. I went in the gym and shot a few jumpers.

He came back into the gym with his son walking beside him. I had no idea what was about to go down. He looked me in the eye and said, "He's yours. You're good, and I know it. I just gotta let go and let you coach him. It's hard to do that sometimes. But you're my guy." Then he looked at his son and said, "This is your coach. He's going to get you where I can't. Where you wanna go. If I say something different than him, listen to *him*. He's right." He looked back at me. "He's yours. And I wanted both of you to hear that from me."

I thanked him and told him I understood. And that I appreciated his transparency and openness to put our conflict on the table, instead of holding it in and letting it fester. We shook hands, and he stayed true to his word, understanding that there was more than one way to play basketball and sometimes two good coaches will have different philosophies, and that's cool. Neither of them will be necessarily wrong.

After our confrontation, his son played even better. By the end of the year, he was our best player, earning All-District honors as a freshman and representing himself and our Warrior Culture well. And his father and I are friends today.

Maybe his son's success was a result of his work and natural development. But it could've been more than that. Maybe this 15-year-old boy, who loved his father more than anyone in the world, could feel the day his dad officially bought into what we were doing. Maybe he could officially trust us because he didn't have a competing voice at home anymore. Whatever it was, his father showed the Warrior Spirit that day. He confronted a problem eye to eye, was self-aware and self-corrected, and sacrificed his ego for the good of the team. And as a result, his son's rate of improvement skyrocketed.

Real influence doesn't happen without reciprocated love. Young kids follow the example of the people they love the most, and the people who love them the most.

Coaching the sons and daughters of coaches can be tough. And honestly, almost every sports fan in the world is an armchair coach. That's simply reality. Knowing this, recruiting the parents to co-opt the Warrior Way with us may be one of our most effective strategies in building a team of Warriors. If our parents can say, "GOOD." Our players will be more likely to be "GOOD."

One of the best Warriors we coached at Lee had a disappointing career from a statistical standpoint through absolutely no fault of his own. He was a highly coveted JUCO transfer with a sweet stroke. Honestly, he was probably above us. We were lucky to have him.

He got off to a great start but got very sick early in his first season as a Flame. He lost over 20 pounds while the illness ran his course. When he finally got himself back into playing shape, he suffered a season-ending ankle sprain.

The next year, he dealt with nagging injuries. And his role became the team tough guy who'd guard anyone. He was an unbelievable teammate. For a guy who had every legitimate excuse in the book to be jaded, he beamed optimism. Any time our team was facing adversity, he was there to project a positive approach, inspiring his buddies to get back up and do their part to right the ship. If he played a lot, he worked. If his minutes were down, he worked.

During his Senior year, Tommy, our head coach, received an email from his father. He paused for a moment before he opened it. When you love and respect a player as much as we did this one, the last thing you want is to get dumped on by their concerned parent. It wouldn't affect our respect for him. If anything, it would've made us respect him even more because he overcame entitled genes.

The entire content of his father's email was gratitude. Our player's Warrior Spirit now made perfect sense. Thanks to the guidance of his Warrior mentor, his dad, he had tapped into it before he came to Lee, while he was with us, and even today. Color me not shocked.

The greatest Warriors we will ever coach will often have Warrior parents. We need to articulate this in a way that doesn't come off as us telling them how to raise their kids. Everyone who has kids knows how hard it is to raise them. Because every kid is different and every family dynamic is unique, no one has cornered the market on universally beneficial parenting practices. So who are we to tell them how to raise their kids?

But we can all agree that being or deciding to adopt the Warrior Spirit as an individual is beneficial. So how can we convey this effectively to our parents to generate trust and buy-in?

This is worth contemplating.

IDEAS

When a parent schedules a meeting expecting conflict, they've probably rehearsed what they're going to say and how they want the conversation to go. Right off the bat, we can pull a quick 180 on this mindset by telling them what we respect about their child and how much we value that.[27] It will reinforce our love and interest in their child and hopefully guide the conversation toward reconciliation instead of dissension.

Many parental conflicts are just a misinterpretation of what's really happening. And sometimes, what's being relayed to mom and dad is far from the truth. The quickest way to get everyone on the same page is to get in a room together and straighten things out. Parents, players, and coaches communicating in truth and working together will enhance accountability.

---

[27] Example: "Lemme start by saying, I love your kid. Johnny shows up every day on time and ready to go. And I know I can count on him."
I know this should go without saying, but just make sure it's true.

Another idea that has worked for us is to make practices open to parents. Some coaches feel differently about this, but as a general rule, inviting parents to observe[28] practice allows them to see the effort that their child is giving and how that stacks up to the other members of the team.

A benefit of open practice is our players get more accustomed to performing in front of an audience. When people come watch us get after it, our players won't feel as much pressure in the games. They get used to eyes on them. We've also found some athletes practice harder if their parent has taken time out of their day to come and watch.

Open practices also give parents an insider's look at how the coaching staff interacts with the team and the planning and passion we put into coaching them.

And most importantly, it allows the parents an illuminating look at Warrior Culture in action. They get to see with their own eyes the optimism, the challenges, the competitive environment, the great teammates, the personal responsibility owned, the excuses rejected, and the truth on display.

---

[28] Observe. Not participate. Make sure before the fact they aren't there to do any coaching. Their child or anyone else's. If we chose to have preseason practices, we must set boundaries to eliminate any distractions.

TELL THE TRUTH. IT DOESN'T JUST HURT, IT HELPS.

Conflict can be uncomfortable, we'll often feel we shouldn't have to justify our coaching decisions to anybody. However, honest discourse benefits all parties involved.

We always consider *our* relationship with the player and with their parents. But sometimes, the relationship that will benefit the most from our truth is the one between the player and their parent.

Imagine we have a second-string player who *is* working hard and doing his best, but his parents think he should be starting. They think it's half our fault for being an idiot coach, and half his fault for being lazy or scared or playing like crap. We know it's neither of those. He simply hasn't won a starting spot yet.

Predictably, they ask for a meeting. We should gladly take 30 minutes out of our day for this if only for the possibility of helping our player at home. We're naïve if we don't realize how difficult these situations are for kids. It's not his fault his parents have unrealistic expectations. And it's not his fault he's not starting yet. This kid is improving and trying his hardest, but he just can't please Mom and Dad.

When we meet with his parents, we'll probably agree to disagree on their kid's talent level, but we can assure them that we think their kid is doing his best, and that we are excited about his improvement. And that we love being his coach. We can encourage patience with the process and celebrate his work ethic.

After hearing all those great things about their kid, how could they still be mad at him? They will probably come to the conclusion that, *Yes. My kid is awesome. But this moron wouldn't know talent if it slapped him in the face.*

Well, that's just fine. Because of an inconvenient 30 minutes in our day, this young man we all love won't have to live in a home where he's a disappointment to his parents anymore. They can be mad at coach all they want, and we should willingly take that on. We don't have to live there. He does.

PART 3:
Competitive Greatness

BUCS: ICE

"The true science of martial arts means practicing them in such a way that they will be useful at any time, and to teach them in such a way that they will be useful in all things."

—Miyamoto Musashi

After our winless football season in 2018, we hired a new head coach, Jeremy Bosken, a U.S. Marine who had been successful turning around struggling high school programs.

Coach Bosken would come to our basketball games. He wanted to watch the players he was about to start coaching get after it. They were becoming Warriors, and he was going to help them take it to the next level.

There was a buzz around the school. A new Warrior Coach was on campus. And Warrior Culture had momentum. You couldn't go to the gym or field or weight room without seeing someone wearing a black "GOOD" T-shirt.

Our men's soccer team, also coached by a U.S. Marine, had been good for a while. I'm sure they were like, "It's about time the rest of y'all showed up."

That summer, Coach Bosken took our strength training to the next level. For a month, our athletes from all sports, male and female, got after it on the field, pushing their bodies further than they ever had. In the weight room, bars clanked on the racks, music blasted from the speakers, and Coach Bosken breathed fire on everyone within earshot.

There were posters on the wall for personal and team records. Athletes received T-shirts for their attendance or specific milestones they achieved. The kids became the Culture. The Culture was now the kids. And the kids were starting to look like anything but kids. They looked like grown athletes who'd stop at nothing while competing. They were becoming Warriors.
It was beautiful.

The next football season, Coach Bosken built on Warrior Culture, introducing the acronym ICE.

It's not about me.
Control the controllable.
Extreme ownership.

He had mostly the same team from the year before. Some of his key players had experienced the competitive advantage of the Warrior Way in basketball, but to the majority of the team, this mentality was new. But they wanted it just like our basketball team had the year before. They wanted to be proud of themselves in the end. They went 8-3 and went out fighting in the playoffs against a very good team. Buc football was back.

Chapter 6

Obsession and Mastery

When I was young, my dad took me to a Bulls game in Indianapolis. Most children are fans of their father's teams and favorite players, and I was no exception.

I hopped in the car wearing my Bulls hat, oversized Bulls Starter jacket, and caricature big head Jordan T-shirt. On the drive to the game, I couldn't contain my excitement. It was the longest two-hour trip I'd ever taken. The game played out in my imagination. I expected Money to drop 50 on the Pacers. I think my dad could feel it. Probably because I hit him with a barrage of *It would be awesome if's* during the first 15 minutes of our trip.

"It would be awesome if Michael makes a game winner."
"... if he has 8 dunks."
"... if he scores 50."
"... if, after the game, we find out he's an alien from another planet."

Dad did his best to help manage my expectations. "Josh, Michael is the best, but people can't ring the bell every night. If he doesn't score 30 points, it's still gonna be great to get to see him play."
He didn't have 50 that night. He had 48.

When I was 17, a family friend had tickets to Game 4 of the NBA finals. He invited me and Dad. It was 1998. *The Last Dance* was playing out in real time. The Bulls won by 4. Rodman had 14 rebounds. Pippen had 28. And Money dropped 34.

The first time I made the trip to spend Christmas with my wife's parents, her father got us tickets to see the Wizards and the Hornets. 38-year-old Money looked like a professional playing against amateurs. The Wizards won by 17. He had 51.
Michael Jordan was a basketball unicorn. And so was his basketball doppelganger.

In the aftermath of the tragedy that claimed the lives of Kobe Bryant, his daughter Gianna, and seven others, people from all walks of life recounted their Kobe story. Each one seemed more incredible, especially when told by the people who knew him best. I watched sports heroes I'd once perceived as invincible weep while talking about Kobe. It was one of those moments where you will remember where you were when it happened. I remember where I was when the jury announced the O.J. verdict, when the towers fell on 9/11, and I'll never forget where I was when I heard Kobe had died.

I spent weeks grieving people I didn't even know personally. It wasn't the loss of a basketball icon that hit me. It was the loss of a person. People. People who weren't even close to being done. People who were becoming.

In basketball, Kobe, like MJ, was a unicorn. Even seasoned professionals with strong work ethic admired his tenacity. The stories of him waking up at 3:00 a.m. to train, often working for 8-10 hours in a day with intermittent breaks. He was blessed with an athletic body that was as close to perfection as any that's existed. The physical limits he defied broke all the rules of training. He under-slept and over-trained, yet got stronger.

One of the most admirable aspects of Kobe's mentality was that his desire to get better burned hottest when he was in his prime. He won five NBA championships and deservedly had placed himself in the GOAT conversation, yet he worked harder.

Physically, Kobe was a unicorn. His body's resilience and his athletic capabilities were in the top 1% of 1% of 1%... and we could probably take that a few levels further. He was a modern-day Hercules.

Mentally, Kobe was born a boy, but he made himself one of the mentally strongest men of our generation, which sort of makes him a mental unicorn, doesn't it? That's what made him and MJ so different. The unicorn status of the physical and the mental materializing in one person.

High-achievers who die young tend to have their legend status elevated above living greats with similar skill sets and career trajectories that we've watched get old. But that doesn't make Kobe or Kurt Cobain or Joan of Arc or Dr. Martin Luther King any less impactful. And I'd venture to guess that as this book ages, the legend of Kobe Bryant will age very well.

Sure, Kobe won the physique birth lottery, but without his mind and personality, he would have just been another all-star athlete. He wouldn't have been recognizable on the mononymous (one-name) level.[29] He wouldn't have become a superstar above superstars. A topical story for motivational speeches. An undeniable option in the water cooler GOAT debate. The player everyone loved, or loved to hate, but left none feeling neutral. The man who transcended race, religion, politics, and even his own sport to bring us together in conversation and sadly, grief.

But physical ability can only take a Warrior so far. And no Warrior we've talked about in this book is without flaws. But their humanity makes them even more inspiring. The 2nd most heartbreaking thing[30] for me about the death of Kobe Bryant is that we wouldn't get to witness and learn from the great things he was poised to do in the next chapter of his life.

His basketball career had ended, but he took the Warrior traits that made him great on the court to life after hoops. His passion, obsession, mental edge, hunger for challenge, competitive spirit, drive to improve translated to the next step on his life's journey.

---

[29] Drake, Madonna, Magic, Shaq, Voltaire, Hannibal, Geronimo, etc.
[30] #girldad

Odds are, our players won't be physical (athletic) unicorns. But they could become mental unicorns. The Warrior Spirit is not some unreachable goal. In fact, it's not even a goal. **The Warrior Spirit is a practice. A way of life that outlives athletic careers.**

Kobe Bryant's ability made him famous. His Warrior Spirit made him Kobe. And this mindset applies to any ventures a person can pursue.

"It's a game. This thing called life. This thing is serious, but it's got a game-like quality to it."

—Kevin Hart

What makes professional athletes different from the rest of the world are their physical gifts that are easy to see with the naked eye.

But what makes guys like Kobe and Michael Jordan different from other professional athletes with similar physical gifts was their obsession with their craft and their drive to be the best. Mental unicorns of obsession, mastery, and competitiveness. It's a rare to see elite physicality combined with elite mentality, but when it happens, posters go up in the rooms of kids who wanna "be like Mike."

Not every person can be blessed with the natural gifts that make them a physical unicorn. But every human being on this planet can tap into the Warrior within them to become a unicorn of the mental game.

This may be another one of my unpopular opinions, but so be it—We all have the Warrior inside us, but somewhere along the way, we forget. We get soft, complacent, lazy, or self-absorbed. When a person realizes that all they need to become the Warrior is already in them, it only comes down to desire. We can have the will, discipline, and resilience required. We just have to decide if we truly desire to be the Warrior.

Becoming a unicorn of the mental game is the Warrior Way. And the Warrior Way enhances our quality of life. That's why there have been a million books written on this topic. Now, a million and one.

But one doesn't become the Warrior by reading books, listening to podcasts, or being inspired by external stimuli. Those things can nudge us in the right direction, sure, but unless it becomes an internal drive, the Warrior Way won't last.

In our adult lives, it's the Warriors that win. They make the most money, the biggest waves in our communities, and the biggest positive impact on the lives of others. At the very least, they live with a quiet confidence and peace, knowing that they are living the best life they can.

Our Warrior Spirit is dying to be released into the wild. We just need to let it out of the prison where our brains, with all our doubt and inhibitions and insecurities, hold it captive.

We don't even have to do anything but have the courage to be who we were made to be. The Warrior within us is enough. People who believe this way are more likely to overcome their fears and be confident. The person who thinks and acts like a Warrior, is a Warrior.

DEATH OF THE ATHLETE

In my coaching career, my reason for coaching (my *why*) has taken many shapes. I guess that's what early career growth looks like. I still remember my first *why—I can't leave the game yet because I still wish I could play. So I guess I'll try this coaching gig.*

It's all I'd ever known. Basketball was my identity. At twenty-two, I knew it was coming. My final season had surpassed all expectation. We were 29-4 and just had to win one last game. And we did.

As with many small college national championship games, there weren't many people in the big arena to witness our triumph. We played our hearts out, and the game was never in doubt. A small crowd of family members, friends, and fans from our school cheered while we got our trophies and banner. We climbed a stepladder to cut down our piece of the net.

I'll never forget. After all the elation and celebratory hugs, I walked alone down the dark tunnel to our dressing room. Many of my teammates were already in there, joking, laughing, and packing their stuff. I sat on a bench and watched them leave one by one. My dad was the last one to leave. He told me he was proud of me. I nodded and said, "Thanks Dad." The door closed behind him. I was alone.

Everything I'd been, all I'd worked for was over. My identity as a basketball player went from prime to flatlined in the second it took the final horn to blow. It was immediately jarring. And in that dressing room, the loss I felt swallowed any happiness I thought this victory would bring.

I wept. Alone.

It felt like a death. And I grieved, spending years in and out of depression. After being a star performing on stage for so long, the volume of my day-to-day life had been turned down to barely audible levels. There were no more adrenaline rush dopamine hits because the crowd went wild. There was a lot of silence, boring work, insignificance, and on my worst days, a loss of relevance I thought I may never achieve again.

During this absurdly quiet spring of 2020, I've remembered moments of greatness past. And to be transparent, I've even had a few moments of grief again. Post-athletic depression is real, especially for those who became Warriors in their sport. Those who knew obsession and gave it their heart and soul only to have their identity stripped away before they reach true adulthood. Even when we know it's coming, it still hurts. Some of us haven't realized that we don't just *get over* the change that the final buzzer brings.

But those who accept this, begin to understand that change in our routines and activities doesn't change our identity. We are not our pursuits. We are still every bit the Warrior we were. That Warrior didn't die. The player did, and we can get better and even move on to something more fulfilling if we can find the will to utilize our understanding of the process of mastery to crush a new passion.

A new passion. That's easier talked about than found. But we must go out and hunt for it. This is of paramount importance. If we don't find our passion, we are at risk of becoming an old, bitter has-been whose loss of relevance enables us to act like a jerk. The kind of has-been that gets jealous of success stories and adopts a cynical view of the intentions of others. Most of us know someone like this. Maybe some of us are like this, and we haven't been able to put our finger on why we feel so angry and bored all the time.

Maybe to be a great coach, we need to be sure that coaching *is* our passion and not just a convenient proxy for a former baller. Because if I've learned anything, a great player and a great coach are two totally different things. The skill sets are different. The approach has to be different. And the motivations have to be different.

For me, when I became a coach was when I finally let the player in me rest in peace. Only to be remembered fondly in two ways:
First, grateful for the fun we had and the mental and physical skills we acquired that transcended our playing career.
Second, understanding what my players may be going through and never forgetting what it was like to be one of them.
Everything else about me as a player was nothing more than ego. And it had to go.

Looking back on the early days of my coaching career, something in me was off. I was a college assistant, fresh off a successful career. I tried to channel my knowledge to inspire the players I coached to become like the player I was. I respected that guy. I knew the success that combination of passion, obsession, work ethic, and toughness could lead to. It could make them beasts. Winners. Warriors. But I was missing something.

My idealistic coaching mentality left little room for flexibility. I had the road map. The plan to greatness, and I shoved it down their throats and shamed the ones who weren't up to the task. The few players I saw myself in loved me as a coach. I don't even want to know what the others thought. It couldn't have been positive. I was like a parent living vicariously through my future pro kid.

The player in me fought to stay alive,[31] or at the least to see himself reincarnated in the game of another. My obsession with basketball was about competing and being a basketball player. It had nothing to do with coaching. Yet, here I was, a coach and a bad one at that. Worse, one who thought he was good and always knew he was right.

So, in 2011, I walked away from the game. My career hadn't taken off like I'd hoped, and I'd found a new

---

[31] Literally. I have been in at least four physical altercations with my players as a college coach. I'm not proud of it. If we're counting other teams, It's at least five. But that one wasn't my fault. I took a punch that was meant for our point guard during a post-game handshake line. Things escalated quickly from there. One day I may tell that story. Today is not that day.

obsession[32] to fill the competitive void that the basketball player in me left post-mortem.
Online poker.

AFTERLIFE: THE TRANSLATABLE HABITS

For twelve years, I made my living playing online poker. In my college days, Friday and Saturday nights meant telling stories and raking in pots with buddies. It was the perfect hobby for a college athlete. It kept me out of trouble. These college home games turned into bigger home games, which—in the most geeky turn of events—led to parking in front of three 30-inch computer monitors for eight hours every day.

Often, people ask me about it—all excited like they just found out I used to work for Al Capone or something. I tell them the truth—the money was nice, the outlet for my competitive drive was great, but it wasn't the glamor show most people think.

Here's what my days looked like:
Wake up, take a shower, and get dressed.
Study. Test hand ranges, run equity calculations, play with decision trees and software with stupid names like Pokerstove and Flopzilla, mull over hundreds of different stats and results based on millions of hands from my database, read articles and forums—riveting stuff, right?

---

[32] A small college assistant basketball coaching salary motivates one to search for a new passion. Especially if you're married with two kids.

Fire up the table scout and hope to find 6 to 10 solid games across multiple sites that have at least one fish (weak player). On the worst days you'll be stuck grinding it out against people with the same skill set as you—except they aren't down-to-earth family guys. Most are internet trolls from 4chan. Lovely bunch.

Check, bet, raise, reraise, minraise, overbet, backraise, click it back, price 'em in, stuff it, and on rare occasions, fold. Head hurt yet? Okay.

Get reads on opponents, battling the same lineups for hours. Some players, you'll battle for months. And on rarer occasions, you'll battle a guy for years, playing tens of thousands of hands against each other.

Your eyes dart from monitor to monitor, table to table, like an erratic dot in a glitchy game of Atari Pong. Stacking fish, engaging in leveling wars with regulars, and on the rarest of occasions, peeing in a bucket.[33]

You close the tables for the day, go to basketball practice, come home and eat dinner. Your kid asks you to play a board game, you oblige. You put on Family Guy and fall asleep, only to do it all over again the next day. Wash—Rinse—Repeat.

Now my head hurts.

The reality—it was as far removed from the Rockstar life of an athlete as you can get. It wasn't remotely athletic, and to this day, it still blows my mind that poker dominated sports channels for so long. It's psychology and high-level math. But I'll tell you this,

---

[33] Don't ask.

the guys who worked at it like I did, got good. Real good.

I don't think I could have become a professional poker player were it not for the skills and thought processes that made me a successful basketball player. There are approaches and habits one can pick up in sports that will translate to competitive greatness across a multitude of fields. Whether it be entrepreneurship, stock trading, coaching, sales, business ownership, poker, or sports, there are certain habits that will give a person the best chance to be successful.

A Deep(er) Hunger for Learning

A growth mindset is a necessary component of success in any field. But there is a difference between success and greatness. One can find success by having an open mind to learn new things presented so they can get better.

One who pursues competitive greatness takes the growth mindset a step further. They don't just accept the truth of the growth mindset.[34] Instead, there is a deeper obsession with acquiring knowledge. Not just knowledge presented to them either. They hunt. They challenge old thoughts. They pursue cutting-edge ideas, sift through them, and fact-check. They find what works best for them because they're open-minded enough to accept that everyone is wired differently.

---

[34] Dweck, Carol S. *Mindset: The New Psychology of Success.* Ballantine Books, 2007.

The path to competitive greatness is a personal pursuit, but it's expedited by feedback from others who have achieved competitive greatness in their craft. Great Competitors find the best and ask them questions. Then they design their own best practices around their unique personality.

I learned that through basketball. After every practice, I would play 1 on 1 with our assistant coach, "Lefty" Glascock. I had immense respect for him. He was a former 2-sport college athlete and played Minor League baseball. He could shoot the heck out of it and was mean as a rattlesnake. He sweat competitive greatness.

After we battled as long as his 45-year-old body would let him. I'd ask him and my dad questions. Often teammates would join in. We'd talk hoops until they made us leave. We learned so much from those talks.

This hunting mentality carried over to poker. I learned from picking the brains of the best daily. The best players I came across did the same. It was like a think tank full of sharks.

Players would post on the forums, asking for thoughts on lines or questions regarding game theory. It was a cool community to be involved in. I remember thinking after a few years as a pro, *No wonder these guys are so good. They're experts, but they're hungry like they're just getting started.*

OBSESSIVE LEVELING UP

In the video gaming community, leveling up is a common concept that makes games more fun. Consider the *Call of Duty* series, a player starts at level one. As their experience and ability grows, they level up, unlocking new skills and weapons to enhance their competitive advantage. Players battle for hours a day not only for the fun of it, but because leveling up your avatar is rewarding. And leveling happens fast in video games.

Some of the most addictive games are RPGs (role-playing games) where the leveling element is the focal point of the game. The game designers have it down to a science. I believe people don't just play video games because they are lazy and want to veg out. It's the leveling aspects that hit the human psyche just right. Getting better is addicting.

Basketball isn't much different. There are two problems many athletes have with leveling up in sports:

First, they don't know how to level up efficiently. The physical changes of their bodies and the experience they gain will help them level up by default, but that won't separate them from the pack, unless they are genetically lucky.

Second, the hard work and dedication required to level up skills is a *slow* process. And some people have a hard time maintaining obsession without immediate results. This is why so many refer to this process as *the grind.*

Personally, I hate that term. It's never a grind when we're doing something we love. But I understand the sentiment. The pay-off is never immediate, but the work is imminent. It takes daily commitment with minimal daily result affirmation, and nothing is guaranteed. But in time, the payoff can be huge.

The parallel is uncanny, even down to the language. Somewhere in the world, an RPG player is *grinding* for skill points so they can level up.

A poker player is *grinding* the virtual felt to build skills and bankroll, hoping to one day be able to do it for a living.

A basketball player is *grinding* in a dimly lit gym, shooting shot after shot, so in three months, three years, or even longer, they can level up and achieve competitive greatness.

All of them can see the big picture. **Few have the will and the stamina to become great.**

Once the Warrior finds knowledge, the real challenge begins—applying knowledge through practice and experience to arrive at higher levels of understanding and ability.

For both the basketball and poker player, this means adding one thing to their game over the course of months. It also may mean eliminating something[35] from their game.

Leveling up never stops. The Warrior doesn't improve as a means to an end. Improvement is a way of life. That's precisely how the Warrior Way

---

[35] a habit that consistently shows poor results or no actual benefit

translates to other pursuits. It's a habit of the mind. How obsessive one is about constantly leveling up in their craft will determine the competitive greatness they achieve further down the path.

EMBRACE COMPETITIVE COMPARISON, REJECT STATUS COMPARISON

Teddy Roosevelt said, "Comparison is the thief of all joy."

I'm sorry Teddy fans, but to me, this is another feel-good, broad-brush, half-true meme quote. Sounds great in a soundbite. Looks great on a motivational poster. But to the Warrior, it's not a universal truth. It's yes and no.

Status comparison, *Up with the Jones's* comparison, comparison that breeds envy and discontentment *is* the thief of all joy. The Warrior rejects that.

But the Warrior might find competitive comparison inspirational, kickstarting the motivational juices of the competitor within, driving the Warrior to outwork their opponents. It causes the Warrior to learn from worthy foes, then strive to beat them.

ATTACH TO QUALITY,
DETACH FROM RESULT

"A man cannot understand the art he is studying if he only looks at the end result without taking the time to delve deeply into the reason of the study."

—Miyamoto Musashi

My friend, Tyler Coston, player development director for PGC uses a great acronym in his shooting talks. NATO—Not Attached To Outcome. This means a player should place great value on the quality of an action regardless of the outcome.

The poker player in me thought, *Beautiful.* I even wrote NATO on a Post-It and smacked it on one of my monitors during my playing days. The truth of this phrase can't be understated when we're dealing with percentage-based activities.

A hitter could predict the pitch, take the perfect cut, knock a frozen rope to the outfield, and be called out when the left fielder makes an unbelievable catch. The outcome was bad. Does this mean the hitter played bad?

I could have a big hand on the turn, make the perfect read, trap my opponent, get all my money into the pot as a 10 to 1 favorite (about as good as you can do in poker), and still lose on the river.[36] Did I play bad?

---

[36] The last community card to come in Texas Hold-Em

A great 3-point shooter will miss 60% of the time. Those 60%, did they shoot bad?

We get it when it's framed like that, but what about when one of our players misses an easy layup or a free-throw? Was that a bad shot? Then why are they being screamed at?

People who are elite in their craft chase quality, not results. They have enough experience to *know* that if the quality is up to their standards, the law of averages will prevail and the results will take care of themselves.

Coaches should do the same. If the quality of the missed layup wasn't up to our standards as a program (i.e. an off-balance prayer in traffic, avoiding contact), then it's time to teach by giving a reminder or technical feedback when we get a chance. But when I see a coach yell at a player who misses a quality attempt, I die a little inside. This coach has forgotten what it's like to be a player.

Nobody, NOBODY in that gym wants to make that layup more than the player who shot it. Missing layups in front of a crowd is embarrassing. The last thing I'd want is my coach grandstanding me in front of my family and classmates, effectively magnifying my incompetence.

Let's call that what it is. A Civilian tantrum by a coach. I've done it. You've probably done it. But it's never changed the result. And we all need to stop. For the sake of the children, stop.

We, as coaches, are professionals. When we act like amateurs, we make it harder for our players. Focus on quality of the action, not the result. It's just what professionals who've achieved competitive greatness do.

Intimidation and Competitive Leveling

From his explosive arrival on the scene in March 1985 at only 18 years of age until his retirement 20 years later, Mike Tyson was the most exciting, intimidating, and at times, disturbing fighter in boxing. He controlled the narrative of the sport for over a decade. It didn't matter who wore the championship belts. Everyone talked about Mike Tyson. He was arguably the most feared fighter of all time.

Most sports fans of the late 80s and 90s have heard variations of this question:

How much money would it take for you to get in the ring with Mike Tyson for one round?

Would you let Mike Tyson punch you in the face for $100K?

Jump in front of a moving truck or fight Mike Tyson?

"Kid Dynamite" won 19 fights in his first year as a pro, all by knockout, and 12 of them in the first round. He won his first Heavyweight title belt against Trevor Berbick. A clip from George Michael Sports Machine's 1986 Plays of the Year will forever be etched in my memory—Berbick went down and stumbled to get up three times while trying to beat the count of referee Mills Lane. I still smile when I think about it.

In George Michael's words, "Trevor Berbick took the longest trip to *The Twilight Zone* I think we've ever seen. It would go on and on... Trevor had a very rough night, folks. If you don't believe it, um... ask him. But he doesn't remember."[37]

My dad loved boxing. In 1988, he somehow finagled his way into a ticket to the Tyson/Michael Spinks championship fight for the lineal heavyweight titles. The story goes that he went to the concession stand for popcorn and a drink. The line was long, and the workers were taking their sweet time. He started to worry he might miss the start of the fight.

As he walked out of the concourse, the crowd erupted. He looked down at the ring. Spinks lay sprawled on the canvas as Tyson walked to his corner. 91 seconds had ticked off the clock in round 1. The fight was over. Dad had made the most rookie mistake you can make at a Tyson fight—miss the first round.

As Tyson matured as a fighter, "Kid Dynamite" became "Iron Mike". No grandiose ring entrances. No fancy trunks. No socks. No flashy robe. He projected irrational confidence and unadulterated rage. His image and reputation instilled fear in his opponents, and most of his fights were over before they began.

That is—until a Tokyo night in 1990 when a desperate James "Buster" Douglas[38] knocked him out in what some call the biggest upset in sports history.

---

[37] www.youtu.be/amtB9MWlauQ
[38] "Buster" Douglas's mother had just passed. Before the fight, he dedicated his performance to her memory. Never underestimate a desperate competitor.

Eight months later, Evander "The Real Deal" Holyfield knocked out an out-of-shape "Buster" Douglas to become Heavyweight champion of the world. This put Tyson and Holyfield on a collision course of epic proportions. It was the fight everyone wanted to see.

But in July 1991, Tyson was arrested on rape charges. And after a lengthy trial, he was sentenced to six years in prison. The fight everyone wanted to see would have to wait.

While Tyson worked out and read books in prison, Holyfield built his own reputation and earned a new nickname. Because of his courage in the ring, "The Real Deal" became "The Warrior". Even when he had a significant size and reach disadvantage, he always leveled the playing field with heart.

Tyson was released in 1995, and Holyfield fought Riddick Bowe for the third time shortly after. Bowe knocked him out in the 8th round. That night, "The Warrior" looked like an old fighter past his prime. But people still wanted to see him fight Tyson. Even Holyfield's mom told him, "You still haven't beat Mike."[39] He was down, but not out.

Tyson was set to fight Peter McNeeley in his return to boxing. The hype around the fight was electric. Nobody gave McNeeley a chance. Rumor has it, even his grandfather bet against him.

---

[39] Holyfield told this story on Mike Tyson's podcast 20 years later. It's an incredible conversation between two old rivals.

But nobody cared that the fight might be lopsided. Everyone just wanted to watch Mike fight again, and I don't think I was alone in thinking he might take out all his anger on this dude with a mullet. I'm not proud of the fact that I wanted to see carnage, blood, and rage. But you know—train wrecks—you gotta look.

As if Tyson wasn't intimidating enough before prison, his ring entrance that night was vintage Mike on steroids, wearing a perma-snarl and his patented towel with a hole cut out of the neck. The band Survivor called it the eye of the tiger for a reason. I thought he wanted to hunt and eat this man.[40]

I remember, as a freshman in high school, watching the fight with my dad and some friends. The room buzzed when we saw Mike's death gaze. While referee Mills Lane gave the fighters their instructions, McNeeley couldn't stand still, swaying, mouth breathing. Mike never moved his head, eyeballs just following—left to right to left to right.

Our room sounded like a choir of baritone "ooh's", and just before Mills Lane shouted, "Let's get it on," McNeeley showed his soul—a fake smile that might as well have spelled the word F-E-A-R across his mouthpiece. You could smell it through the TV. That's all it took. My dad said, "This fight just ended right there."

---

[40] Years later, I realized that I may not have been wrong in my initial assessment.

Boxing isn't a sport for the soft. These men are born and bred fighters. They're all tough guys. Even still, Mike beat *good* boxers before matches ever started with his ability to intimidate. And it wasn't just the boxers he'd intimidate—it was their managers, their corner men, even their friends and family.

Surprising to me. The bell rang, and McNeeley charged him like a mountain ram. Not-so surprising, he hit the canvas after 8 seconds.
"If this was a rodeo, he'd be in good shape," Dad said.
He popped up and ran around the ring, radiating nervous energy. Mills Lane gave the standing eight count. The fight continued.

People like to make fun of McNeeley—the mullet alone makes him an easy target. And this may be another unpopular opinion, But I was impressed with him that night. He went for broke. Despite being afraid and outclassed in every way, he took the fight to Tyson and threw bombs. Most of them missed or glanced off Tyson, who countered with power shots of his own, but that's beside the point.

McNeeley overcame being intimidated and fought with courage. But after a devastating combination put him down again with 1:31 left in round 1, his trainer, Vinnie Vecchnione, who may or may not have soiled himself during Lane's fight instructions, panicked. McNeeley was wobbly, sure, but he wanted to continue. And the best referee in boxing would've let him, but Vecchnione entered the ring and stopped the fight.

McNeeley looked upset with his trainer. He probably didn't want to go out on his shield, but he wanted to finish the fight his way. And maybe he just wanted to give the fans a chance to get what they wanted—their money's worth, or in my case, a little blood.

Panic. Anyone is susceptible if they get intimidated, even rough mafia wise guys like Vinnie Vecchnione. Tyson said it himself, "Everyone has a plan until they get punched in the face." The grand master of intimidating arts would know.

Tyson rolled through his next three opponents in 7 rounds combined and looked better than he did before he went to prison.

Next up—Evander "The Warrior" Holyfield—a man not even Genghis Khan with his Mongolian hoarde could intimidate. But Tyson stuck to his plan. He'd change for no one. In his mind, he'd get him just like he had everyone else.
But then, he got punched in the face... And we know the rest of that story.

Back when I would frequent the casinos to play in live poker tournaments, it was easy to tell who was who. There's a quote from the movie *Rounders* that says, "If you can't spot the sucker in the first half hour at the table, then you are the sucker."[41]

It's true. Often, a pro can tell if a player is good by how they shuffle their chips, or how they look at their

---

[41] *Rounders.* Directed by John Dahl, written by David Levian and Brian Koppelman, performance by Matt Damon, Miramax Films, 1998.

cards, or their poker terminology, or even by their conversation or the look in their eye.

In sports, there are a lot of "suckers". This is great news for us as coaches. We just have to motivate our players to work hard so they can be more skilled than most. When we're more skilled, we win, right? It shouldn't be that difficult.

The problem is—sports don't happen in a vacuum, nor are the games played in theory.

This is where variables—the human elements we have been writing about, microgame[42] and metagame[43] skills, and the mental game—come in to play. Who's tougher? Who has better strategy? Who plays better as a team? Who has matchup advantages? Who's the most desperate to win? And something we rarely think about—Who's at risk of being intimidated?

Let's consider that last one. I think intimidation is a bigger deal in high school sports than people realize. Think about it—Our players are not far removed from being a card-carrying member of humanity's most likely-to-be-intimidated age group, middle schoolers.

We see pecking orders and pack mentality at all stages of life, but nowhere is it more on-the-nose than middle school. I imagine most high school kids are still battling their intimidation factor,[44] they just get better at hiding it.

---

[42] The games within the game.
[43] The long-term adjustment game.
[44] Likelihood of bowing to a capable foe who is irrationally confident.

In poker, we had this concept between pros called a leveling war.[45] Rather than explain it I'll show what leveling looks like.

Level 1: *I think.*
Level 2: *I think he thinks*
Level 3: *I think he thinks that I think*
Level 4: *I think he thinks that I think that he thinks*
Level 5: *I think he thinks that I think that he thinks that I think*

These psychological levels are correlated to a player's ability. Judging by their play, one can accurately assess what level they are on mentally. For example, level 1 poker players might as well be wearing their cards on their forehead. Not only do they suck at the game, but they can't hide how they feel about their hand.

Level 2 players will pose every time. If they look strong, they're weak, and vice versa. They will also be friendly with better players, giving up on pots they should fight for because they feel like they're outclassed.

Level 3 players base their game on hope and attempt to manipulate their opponent with reverse level 2 psychology. They'll act strong when strong. And weak when weak, hoping the good player will think they're on level 2. But the better player sees through this facade. Level 3s try their best, but don't have the chops to compete against better players. And although they think they're playing their best, they end up putting

---

[45] Not like the *leveling up* concept we addressed earlier, but figuring out what cognitive level your opponent's thought process is on.

their stack on the line on a gamble, giving up to hope. As Kurt Vonnegut says, "And so it goes."

Level 5 was all I needed most times. But I'll admit, I've been leveled by great players who thought on a deeper level. "GOOD"—that just meant it was time to get better.

Similar to poker, I believe there are psychological levels in the mental warfare between athletes and teams that are correlated to their talent level. For the sake of simplicity, Let's put a hard cap at 5 levels while we look at leveling from the team sports perspective.

Level 1: *We suck. We can lay down. It doesn't matter. Our efforts are futile.*
Level 2: *We think we're good. But if they're better, they can have it.*
Level 3: *We're good. We hope we can beat them.*
Level 4: *Nobody is better than us. We'll crush anyone standing in our way.*
Level 5: *We've done everything in our power to be great at this. We don't care who they are. We just want a great fight.*

Let's unpack this and make it useful for our teams.

Level 1: We suck. We can lay down. It doesn't matter. Our efforts are futile.
Let's assume for a moment that if you're reading this, your program isn't a level 1. Everyone has teams in their league that are level 1s. We schedule the games. We get better in practice without taking them into consideration because they aren't a threat. We just try to get through the games without creating bad habits or getting anyone hurt.

When playing these teams—it's a bad idea to oversell the level 1 opponent. It insults the intelligence of our players and is a massive disconnect that could become a coach's worst nightmare—a running locker room joke.

Now, if we feel like our team is a level 1. We need to pour every ounce of energy into improving the strength and skill of our players, developing them while keeping it fun.[46] It doesn't matter what we do if our players aren't good enough and can't enjoy it enough to care.

If our players don't care and won't work to get better, we have 3 choices:
Find new players.
Find a new job.
Be a great teacher and quit caring so much about the results of our games. Teach players good habits, do it for the stipend, and let everyone have an enjoyable time.

Level 2: We think we're good. But if they're better, they can have it.
The vast majority of sports programs are level 2 or 3. The problem with the level 2 team is that they *think* they're good but have a weak competitive drive. It's unlikely that a team can be good without being highly competitive. Honestly, I respect level 1 teams more than level 2s. At least they have the integrity to admit they aren't good. I've coached a few level 2s. It didn't go well. It's hard to coach people I don't respect.

---

[46] And spend a ton of time with the youngest athletes in your school.

There are two types of players competitive coaches don't get along with—soft and selfish. If there are soft or selfish players in our program, we have to *show* them the truth every chance we get. They'll make that job easy because they can't help but reveal themselves. We just gotta catch it on film or in practice. Then meet with them 1 on 1 in the most nonthreatening way possible. I've learned that if we come at them guns blazing in public, they'll go into defense mode. And we'll be less likely to reach them.

I'm not sure any athlete consciously wants to be known as soft or selfish. But, of course, many act otherwise. We have to find out who they want to be, show them how their actions aren't aligned with that, and hold them the standard of the person they want to become. But if they refuse to change, or they live in denial—We have to show them the door. It may cause a few short-term headaches and a parent meeting, but our team and our sanity will go to a much better place.

Hopefully, players who can't refuse to get outside themselves will leave on their own. But it doesn't always play out like that. And soft, selfish players make coaching an exercise in misery. No amount of short-term success is worth it.

I took a hiatus from coaching once. It was the day I realized I was going to have to coach players I didn't like for another year. So I walked away. But the game pulls you back in when it lives it in your soul. But on my return, I decided I'll never coach another player I don't like.

It's not always easy, and we might have to pull a painful splinter from our team's proverbial butt, but—at the risk of coming off cliche—it's addition by subtraction. Subtracting a negative. That's just good math. And it's okay that not everyone will understand. If we want our program to be special, only Warriors get to sit in our lockers. And only Warriors will understand. The soft ones, the selfish ones, they need to transfer to a level 2 where those qualities are acceptable.

Or they need to resign.

Or get resigned.

There is a dangerous thought that exists in athletes that perfectly describes a level 2 competitor, *If I don't try that hard, I won't have to face the truth that I'm not good enough.* That's so dangerous because weak logic can spread to impressionable people.

Level 3: *We're good. We hope we can beat them.*
In my opinion, Peter McNeeley was a level 3. He was a good boxer who had a respectable career, but he knew his physical skills were capped and he hoped he could win. He tried but wasn't good enough. This is a respectable place to be. It's not the next two levels, but many Warriors who come up short have this mentality.

They know their ability is limited because they're smart and objective. Self-aware. Because of this, they manage their expectations. Protecting themselves. They limit their dreams with rationality and logic—not that there's anything wrong with that—but they don't become great. One who dares to dream big enough, giving them a chance to defy the odds to accomplish something astounding, no matter how small the chance may be. Against better opponents, they won't let themselves truly believe.

Bettors in Vegas love these teams. They beat the teams they're better than, win around half the time against teams with similar abilities, and rarely beat teams better than them. They don't shock the world. They remain nameless. Respectable, but boring.

Level 4: *Nobody is better than us. We'll crush anyone standing in our way.*

Beware of Dog. I consider Mike Tyson the baddest level 4 in professional sports history. But there is a problem with level 4s, even one as talented as Tyson.

At some point, they'll come across someone they can't intimidate—The bad matchup who won't back down. Evander Holyfield was that guy to Mike—the dangerous combination of strength, skill, and will. In their first fight, Tyson couldn't hurt him, and the underdog Holyfield knocked him out in the 10th round.

The rematch looked to be more of the same. Holyfield controlled the early action. Tyson couldn't get to him and didn't know what to do. Then he found a way out. He got frustrated with an unintentional headbutt from Holyfield, threw a fit, and bit off a chunk of Holyfield's ear. Not once, but twice. Referee Mills Lane disqualified him. As entourages and randoms entered the ring, an angry, embarrassed "Iron Mike" led the charge in a full-scale brouhaha. It was pandemonium. The epitome of "you-better-be-glad-their-holdin'-me-back" fake toughness.

Tyson carried himself with irrational confidence, but he didn't adjust to Holyfield when he couldn't bulldoze him. His strategy was weak, and he had no back-up plan. But there may have been something else at play. Something invisible to the untrained eye. Something missing that every true Warrior must have in their soul.

Tyson's former trainer, the great Teddy Atlas, articulated this as well as anyone ever has on Joe Rogan's podcast. "He (Tyson) knew he wasn't that guy, and when you're not that guy, guess what—you have a great talent of recognizing when somebody is."[47]

Whoa. Take a moment to let that sink in.

When people know they aren't Warriors, they're experts at recognizing who is. That sentence sums up intimidation. Everyone's going to run into that man, that woman, that team, that difficult life situation that will test our limits. Irrational confidence and our ability to intimidate won't be enough. Skills aren't enough. Speed isn't enough. Money won't be enough.

We have to *know* the Warrior Spirit is in us. We have to *know* we are resilient. We have to *know* we thrive in a difficult fight. We have to *know* we are the Warrior. If we don't *know*, we have a problem.

Level 5: *We've done everything in our power to be great at this. We don't care who they are. We want a great fight.*

---

[47] Teddy Atlas on the Joe Rogan Experience MMA Show #42

The Holy Grail of Confidence. This is Warrior territory, where there is no entitlement, only work, passion, obsession, and pride. It's a confidence earned, and a confidence owned. An important part of coaching is to inspire our best players to pursue this level. This is Evander "The Real Deal" Holyfield, "The Warrior."

This person exceeds all expectations. They hit, get hit, and hit harder back. They go down. They get up swinging. This player is revered by their coaches, years after their careers are over. They love the battle more than the result. If they can avoid emotional setbacks, this team beats everyone weaker, everyone as good, some that are better, and on special nights, they shock their state and achieve what the sportswriters thought impossible. This Warrior amazes historians, is loved by many, and respected by all.

GREATNESS IS AND ISN'T ALL-INCLUSIVE

Because the world is full of unique personalities who pursue different passions, it might be best that we don't project our idealistic approaches to competitive greatness in our craft onto people who dabble but don't care to achieve that level.

I've found that since most high school players are recreational, less[48] is often more.[49] For example: Practices over 2 hours are brutal for high school kids.

---

[48] Time and information
[49] Quality, efficiency, and energy.

They have been at school for 7 hours and often have homework when they finally walk into their bedroom. That can be tiring even when they're fresh. With our college teams at Lee, we rarely had a 2nd semester practice over 90 minutes. During the meat of our conference schedule, we usually went a shade over an hour. We found that our players were healthier and fresher, mentally and physically, by tournament time.

The thing is, there may be 1 in 1,000 high school players[50] who, if everyone's being honest, want to achieve competitive greatness in basketball. And there is a chance that one player would feel differently if they really knew the difficulty of the process and what they would have to sacrifice in order to be great at high levels.

Competitive Greatness is a fascinating and rewarding pursuit. But it comes with a price for those who chase it. And the vast majority of people (especially teenagers) aren't willing to pay that price. Is it fair to ask our players to work out like Damian Lillard or Kobe? If we did, I'd bet it would lead to burnout in most cases.

Just because most of our players won't care to achieve competitive greatness by obsessing about our sport, doesn't mean they don't want to good at it. It also doesn't mean they don't want to be Warriors. It probably means they're more self-aware than we

---

[50] In my opinion, this is a low estimate. And no, we're not above making up stats on the spot. We are coaches. It's kind of our thing.

think. Deep in their sub-conscious, they may know how far this game can take them. And they might even know they won't be playing it longer than five more years at the most. They want to get good simply so they can enjoy it more. Not so they can be the best.

I used to get so frustrated because my players didn't want to work on their game all the time like I did. And then when we'd lose a tough one, I'd shame them about it. That wasn't coaching. That was anger about the loss combined with the damage it did to my ego.

Every once in a while, we may have a player who will chase competitive greatness. That player will study, obsess, relentlessly pursue mastery, and be borderline OCD about it. And they would do all that with or without our help. There will be rewards for this player, but there will also be a price. If you don't believe me, ask anyone who's done it.

I wonder if Michael Jordan had many friends.
I wonder if Kobe had to make sacrifices in his family life to do what he did.
I wonder how many ex-NFL players struggle with the aftermath of CTE.
I wonder how many ex-Olympic medalists suffer from post-athletic depression.
I wonder how many pro poker players feel sub-human because they disconnected from their emotions for so long.
I wonder how many older E-Sports star deal with the pain of carpal tunnel.
I wonder how many great high school prospects sacrificed their prom to play AAU.

I wonder why, at 40, I haven't walked up stairs without knee pain in over a decade.

Most people aren't willing to make sacrifices to achieve competitive greatness in something as finite as a basketball career. But many of those same people *will* have a burning desire to be great at something that will last longer, or will make them more money, or will be more suited to their natural abilities.

We shouldn't expect our players to obsess about our sport. But we can expect our players to be Warriors while they're with us. And to work hard to be as good as they can be at this sport they have chosen. But their life doesn't have to revolve around something that's short-term passion for them.

The Warrior Spirit leads to a rewarding life. And the only cost is the work it takes to be a strong person. And that work becomes the reward itself.

Chapter 7

The Invisible

"Perceive that which cannot be seen by the eye."
—Miyamoto Musashi

A MEME AND ITS MANY variations surfaced in the mid-2000s that never failed to make me chuckle. A photo of an empty field, school hall, or living room with a caption that stated, "There are four Ninjas in this picture."
One showed an empty city street captioned, "17th annual Ninja parade."

The Ninja (Hollywood name) or Shinobi (historically accurate name) were spies and assassins in 15th century Japan. In recent times they have become media darlings in movies and video games because of their sleek look and ambiguous nature.

But real Ninjas didn't look like Bruce Lee or Chuck Norris. They didn't wear masks or dress in black. They looked like normal every-day people, blacksmiths, merchants, or monks because that's who they were. And blending into their surroundings made them invisible. A target never saw them... until it was too late.

The first Ninjas in recorded history were the Iga-Ryu clan and the Koga-Ryu clan. Their villages were protected by mountainous terrain and rivers. Isolated in their respective villages, their children trained in secret.

After years of rigorous training in martial arts, stealth tactics, survival, food and sleep deprivation, and athletic training such as mountain climbing, the young adult would become the Ninja.

By the time a Ninja took their first mission, they were as well trained as any Warrior in history. They worked alone, allowing for maximum stealth. They practiced mindfulness and meditation, learning many esoteric feats the human body is capable of.

Utilizing their imaginations, they crafted outside-the-box weapons from the limited resources in the villages. Weapons like the Makibishi,[51] the Shuriken,[52] and smoke bombs. Ninjas spent years mastering their skills[53] and the tools at their disposal before they took them into calculated combat.

---

[51] Dark spikes they threw on the ground behind them while being pursued.
[52] Not the Ninja stars Hollywood invented, these were hidden hand blades.
[53] Ninjitsu.

As mercenaries, Ninjas were different. They were about survival. They had a code, but it was very abstract and, in stark contrast to the Bushido code of the Samurai, dealt more with tactics than morality. The Samurai looked down on the Ninja because of the Ninja's backhanded stealth tactics and the class difference between these two types of Warriors. The Ninja didn't care, their tactics were how they made a living. For them, morality was survival, and a Warrior clan does what it must, as best they can, to survive.

Ninjas were so good at their jobs, that many high-profile Samurai who considered themselves targets for a Ninja assassin would fortify their residences with anti-Ninja measures. But more often than not, these measures were no match for the Ninja who would strike from the shadows, leaving in their wake a terrifying question, how?

The untrained eye often doesn't always understand how the Warrior does it. But experts know full well. They see past physical tools and skill sets. They see the unseen. Many of these experts are holding college scholarships. They're looking for Warriors.

Our players need to know that if they want to be noticed by the experts. They need to put a premium on things invisible to the common fan. Training. Intangibles. Will to win. Poise.

THE INVISIBLES: TRAINING

There are common themes the Warrior Cultures of history share, but none more obvious than work ethic. It's easily articulated but difficult to do. It's easy to preach but hard to practice. And one step further, it's easier to own than it is to inspire in others.

The most effective use of a strong work ethic has become a hot debate in our sports culture. Many days, my social media feeds consist of the "train more" crowd engaged in heated arguments with the "play more games" crowd.

The thing is, the sharpest minds (players, coaches, and analysts) don't pick a side. They understand the value of both aspects of development—the balance of skills training with the experience of competition. It's discouraging that such arguments even exist.

It may be a microcosm of a problem in today's youth sports landscape[54]—most people engaged in this argument, well-intentioned as they believe they are, have an agenda. The personal trainer wants more personal training. They AAU coach or tournament director thinks more competition and games is the way to go.

Personally, I lose respect for anyone who argues for one against the other. Both are needed, equally, and as often as possible. Players need repetition to master

---

[54] The problem goes deeper than athletic development. Information, whether truth or fallacy, that people are likely to push onto others often serves a narrative that serves their self-interests.

skill. They also need competition to experiment and hone their skills in games.

Boxers don't just hit the speed bag all day and do push-ups. They spar. Soldiers don't just shoot at targets all day. They do team exercises and real-time simulations. A Warrior must train their skills relentlessly, then they need to scrimmage.

We see this in coaching so often, and at certain points in our careers, maybe we've been guilty of picking one side over the other. Some coaches will run players through drills for an entire practice. Some will scrimmage all day. The best will be found somewhere in the middle.

There is wisdom on both sides. The trainer understands that **most novices confuse capability with mastery.**
The "more games" coach understands that **complete mastery cannot occur without the application of skills in competitive scenarios.**

A skill isn't fully realized until it can be performed without thought.[55] And the confidence needed to peak-perform isn't obtained until those skills are consistently demonstrated when the stakes are high.

When we find ourselves in an asinine argument such as this, it's probably best to paint our view gray and seek the promised land that is *the best of both worlds.*

---

[55] Unconscious competence from the four stages of competence. Broadwell, Martin M. (20 February 1969). "Teaching for Learning (XVI)" wordsfitlyspoken.org. The Gospel Guardian.

So, how did these poor, rural village folk of the Japanese mountains become one of the most skillful Warrior Cultures in human history?

They trained *and* competed. Picture a young child, practicing a move. Rep after rep. For years.

It was a lifestyle.

Bruce Lee, the most famous modern Ninja, trained relentlessly in martial arts, studied Warrior Cultures, and became one of the most quotable Warrior philosophers or our time.

Okay, he wasn't actually a Warrior, but he understood the Warrior Way and could articulate it pretty well. He said, "Do not fear the man who has practiced 10,000 kicks. Fear the man who has practiced one kick 10,000 times."

History doesn't tell us exactly how Ninjas became fighting legends. But my guess—Ninjas sparred and played hundreds, maybe thousands, of mini-games before they snuck in a building for an actual game.

In the same vein as martial arts, Basketball is a technique game. And there is a prerequisite for a player to have any chance at success—They must achieve a level of mastery over the ball. This is dribbling, passing, and shooting.

Shooting is the most under-trained skill in basketball. Some might argue that we train shooting more than anything else. I might be inclined to agree, but I also advocate for more shooting training to achieve the level of mastery required to win any game of real significance.

Take the skill of rebounding as an example. I've heard great coaches say, "Defense wins games. Rebounding wins championships." And... "Two stats can explain your wins and losses, turnovers and rebounding."

Sounds important. While these quotes are gross minimalizations of what happens in a game, I partly agree with both statements. So why don't we train rebounding more?

Because it's freaking easy.

Shot goes up, find an opponent and get them out of the area. Find the ball. Go get the ball. It's that simple. It's a novice skill. But people forget novice skills if they aren't habitual, and that is why, unfortunately, we have to waste small amounts of our practice time working on it. One interesting thing we've figured out, the tougher our team, the less we have to work on rebounding.

What about ball handling? Well, in my personal experience, I mastered dribbling by 7th grade. I've also seen 7-year-olds on Instagram that have achieved a high level of mastery.

This might be an unpopular opinion too, but I think dribbling is the most over-trained skill in basketball. I'm not trying to say it's easy, but it took me about 4 years, doing drills for 10-15 minutes a day and playing a ton of basketball in the rec center gym, in the driveway, and anywhere else I could find a goal and a friend to play with.

7-year-olds can master dribbling. I'm not saying it's easy, I'm just saying... 7-year-olds.

Dribbling skill is just a part of ball handling. Passing is ball handling (under-trained). The position you play from while holding the ball is ball handling (under-emphasized). Receiving a pass is ball handling. Getting open on the wing or in the post is a deeper concept of ball handling.

Any micro skill that limits our team's turnovers and allows us to keep control of the ball can be considered ball handling. The best way to get better at ball handling is to be aware of these little things and technically apply a good fundamental approach in games. It's not just about dribbling in place. Maybe it's not about that at all.

But shooting. The impact of the glorification of dribbling has left our game with a multitude of high school and college players with superfluous handles who can't shoot.

Most days, I wish our training regimens placed a premium on shooting and left most, if not all, of the ball handling work to game experience. Shooting is the most difficult skill to master. Bruce Lee might say it's the kick that needs to be practiced 10,000 times. And someone who knows what it takes to be a great shooter might say that number should be multiplied by 100. But how many kids are shooting even 10,000 shots on their own in a month of workouts?

There isn't immediate glory in shooting the same shots the same way in an empty gym to achieve that level of mastery. Instagram and twitter won't care. It won't get likes, and our followers will most likely get bored and move on to Rex Chapman's block or charge videos.

But that's what I love about the Ninjas. They trained for years on their own. In private. Unseen by anyone outside their village. Not for pats on the back, but for preparation. They didn't do it so people could see them working. They trained to become great at what they did.

It takes intense daily mental focus and physical discipline to become *great* at something. But it also takes complete understanding of the game and the skills that will lead to the most success. And it takes significantly more time than you can advertise on social media.

In a world where altruism is gradually falling to virtue signaling, the Warrior doesn't follow the trends. They understand that the most growth takes place alone. On their own time. In a dimly lit gym. In an old weight room. On a field with a buddy. In a private space behind stacks of books and a monitor with a dozen open research tabs. On a beach with their boat crew.

It's a lifestyle. No cameras. The local news won't show up. **Those willing to work in the dark will gain a significant advantage over their competition.**

Ninjas trained in the shadows of Japan, mastering their craft to become the greatest assassins the world has ever known. To gain the skills they needed to survive. And without trying, they became legends. If Chuck Norris is our go-to tough guy. The Shinobi are Chuck's.

THE INVISIBLES: INTANGIBLES

Becoming a master of a craft isn't as simple as acquiring the tools of the trade. It requires wisdom. Basketball has a flow to it. It's an art form. A player must know when to employ a skill and when to show restraint. And how to use their skills to enhance the skills of their teammates.

To become a master of the game, one must become an artist. One doesn't become an artist with theory and technique alone. It takes a higher understanding of the nuance and variables within the game. A vision on the court that the common fan, and most players, don't see. In basketball terms, we call this court vision. And people who understand basketball know that court vision is not just a term about passing the ball. It's about feel.

Intangibles are reflections of character in action. Warriors understand that their character, above all, will enhance their feel for the game. And this feel sets the bar for their competitive potential.

College recruiters place a premium on intangibles because intangibles directly correlate to a high rate of improvement *and* good team chemistry. Both of which often dictate whether a team will have a winning season or a disappointing grind through frustration. Winning seasons allow college coaches to keep their jobs or get better jobs. They recognize that intangibles put food on their table and Christmas presents under their tree. Winning intangibles like to live in Warrior Cultures. Here's a short list of intangibles college coaches are looking for that we should share with our players:

Enthusiasm

Effective Communication

Preparation

Daily Work Ethic

Playing Hard

Fundamental Precision

Encouragement

Confident, Respectful, and Empowering Body Language

High Fives, Chest Bumps, and Authentic Celebration

Intense Focus

Personal Responsibility

Treating Each Other with Respect (Eye Contact)

Telling the Truth

Accepting the Truth

Sharing the Ball

Dropping the Arrogant Side of the Ego

Dependability

Attention to the Little Things (Details)

Rejecting the Urge to Blame

Owning Failure

Resilience

Resilience

Resilience

Resilience

Resilience

Resilience

Resilience

Resilience

Resilience

Resilience

The Invisibles: Will

In the movie *Braveheart*,[56] Hollywood took many creative liberties with the account of Scotland's fight for freedom, Mel Gibson's character is actually mixed-mash story of William Wallace *and* Robert the Bruce. But hey, Shakespeare didn't let facts hinder his stories either. So, I'll give *Braveheart* a pass. It gets a pass in my book because I liked the movie. If I'd hated it, I imagine I'd feel differently and critique its inaccuracies with more than a dash of vitriol. What isn't up for debate, is that William Wallace possessed a strong will and inspired his people to escape the oppressive rule of the English crown.

172 years after the death of William Wallace, 15th century Scottish poet Blind Harry wrote a long poem, *The Wallace*, that became a patriotic legend, despite its historical inaccuracy. This poem was the inspiration for *Braveheart*.
But history tells a slightly different story.

Wallace led the armies of the Scottish uprising for seven years. But while he chalked up victories and fame, his ego and anger grew alongside his reputation. Feeling invincible, his raids became barbaric as he razed English settlements, murdering even the women and children. Ego and anger were the variables that would undermine his military career and result in his defeat at the Battle of Falkirk, where he threw out strategy and tried to win with brute force. His Scottish forces bull rushed an English army more than twice their size. Over 10,000 Scots died on that

---

[56] *Braveheart*. Directed by Mel Gibson, Paramount, 1995.

battlefield, and the heralded hero of Scotland narrowly escaped death, but he didn't escape disgrace. The Scottish nobles who had grown tired of Wallace, betrayed him to the English. And he was tortured and executed more brutally than the movie depicted.

No matter how strong the Warrior, rage and ego compromise the will to win. In sports, it's called **poise**. While victors show poise time after time, many careers end when talented players are found lacking.

William Wallace was a determined man of exceptional ability. But again history tells us that skill isn't enough. Will isn't enough. A Warrior must always keep their poise.

Will. What exactly does that mean?
We know, sure, but can we articulate it?
Working with high school students every day, I've learned it doesn't matter what we know if we can't articulate it to our athletes. And I'd go one step further—we need to articulate it in a way that inspires them to action.

Will—the faculty by which a person decides on and initiates action. It can be exerted to achieve something or restrained to control one's impulses.

Interesting. So, when we say a player has the *will* to win, we mean—the player decides (and it *is* a decision) to exert their faculty (in this case—determination and ability) to achieve the win.
Like this:
decision + (Determination)(Ability) = result

Let's break this equation down to parts we can apply to our team.

Decisions

We can decide all we want, but our decision is irrelevant if we don't have the Determination or the Ability to execute it. We've already discussed that the Warriors have decided ahead of time how they will act before they have to act. But basketball happens so fast that decisions and actions must be instinctual. There is no time to think about it.

Therefore, decision-making and ability have a symbiotic relationship. As we've mentioned earlier, competence is correlated to the speed of decision-making. A high skill level that is instinctual (habitual) will greatly enhance performance.

Determination

Strength in this area can be gained by devising plans and creating good work habits to achieve said plans. Great players are intentional about their plans to improve and their determination to put it into action every day.

Unfortunately, some high school players show a gross lack of determination to do much of anything.
That's not a judgement. It's an observation. They have to be pushed and prodded along every step. We try to get them to do something that we consider valuable. They don't see it that way. It's not in them. We want to pull our hair out.

As a coach, we have four options here:

Find a way to inspire them.[57]

Give them the opportunity (Read: advise them) to play a different sport. Or just cut them.

Make everyone's life miserable by yelling and complaining all the time.

Or stop pretending like we care. Let them have a good time sitting on the bench and utilize their skills only if the team really needs it.

Ability

All people are created equal. All athletes are NOT. As coaches, we know this, but for some reason, we have a hard time coming to terms with it.

We build our culture, implement X's and O's, teach defensive strategy, and make scouting reports. It's easy to get caught up in strategy. But we have to remember, again I'm reminding myself here, it's our job to help our players get better every day. Improved ability will increase confidence, work ethic, and the effectiveness of determination.

The team with the most ability usually wins. So we must be intentional about helping our players improve their skills daily. One of the most effective things we can do as a basketball coach is set aside a block of practice for player development each day.

---

[57] Our methods will be not be the same for every player because each personality is motivated differently. Motivation isn't one-size-fits-all. It is dynamic. And we need to understand our player's personalities to motivate effectively.

We multiply ability and determination in our equation because their value goes up when they coexist.

This may seem a little obvious, but I know coaches who can't figure out why certain players don't have the drive to work on their games. To us, the answer is usually a blunt one, but we'll phrase it gently. Those players suck at basketball.

But if we can help those players find the initial drive to work through the suck (the times when they're over-matched or under-skilled), they'll find themselves getting better. Their improved abilities will lead to the game becoming more fun. When ability goes up, fun goes up. When fun goes up, determination goes up. Our players need to know this.

Big-time determination is earned by working through hard times when tangible results seem so far out of reach. The Warrior Spirit says, "Hard times? GOOD." Players who aren't good enough yet need encouragement (especially from older peers) and reminders (from coaches) that the process doesn't happen overnight. A team of Warriors celebrates the struggle. They know if their buddies can hang in there, it *will* get better. *They* will get better.

When they eventually see a result like a personal record in the weight room, then they'll spend more time in the weight room, gaining more strength which will lead to more ability. Maybe after a few hot shooting days, they'll get in the gym more, which will lead to more ability. Slowly, they'll *feel* themselves improving. When players see results, they want to do it more. Remember, getting good at something (leveling up) is fun and addicting.

Disenfranchised Players, Thanks Coach.

Guiding and encouraging our players through the reality of the improvement process is important, but there's a dark side of this aspect of coaching that we don't talk about much.

Instead of inspiring them to be more determined, we might squelch their determination if we have unrealistic expectations. Unrealistic expectations are immediately demotivating.

Worse, we might paint an unrealistic picture of the career they could have. Unrealistic stories of grandeur take more time to do damage, but they eventually crush the spirit. This kid becomes less and less determined over time, and we might tell their salty parents that we can't make their kid love the game. But the reality is, we sold them a lie.

As hard as it is sometimes, we have to tell the truth *all the time* if we want to avoid curbing their determination. And if we don't know what their career trajectory might look like, we need to keep our projections to ourselves and let the work play out until we can see realistic possibilities.

Again, this may seem obvious, but I see so many youth coaches telling elementary kids they're gonna be D1. Really? Do these coaches realize that there's a baseline of size and athletic ability a player has to have to even have a chance?

If the physical development of one of these "early bloomers" plateaus, they might stop working as hard. And can we blame them? Peers caught up, and "late bloomers" passed them. And they realized that the dream they once had (or had been sold) is dying, and their defense mechanism for that is to stop trying so hard. This is a disenfranchised player.

I've seen this song and dance play out so many times with elementary and middle school stars who became mediocre high school players. Sometimes I wonder if this could be avoided if everyone (parents and coaches) just pumped the brakes on youth career projections. There are just too many unpredictable variables.

So in regards to the present, it's important that we're aware of the limits of our players so we don't ask them to do something they just aren't capable of. Expecting players to consistently perform above their ability does not cultivate fearless performances. It hinders them.

Humans can't run through cinder block walls like the Incredible Hulk no matter how determined one might be to do so. We'd be well served not to expect and ask someone to do something they can't do. If we do, the result is on us. This sounds obvious, but I know I've had unrealistic expectations of players that adversely affected how I treated them.

I once overheard a coach yelling at his dejected 7th grade AAU team in the corner of the gym. They'd just gotten 30-pieced by a team with a 6'7 kid.
7th grade. He was a reclassed redshirt.

His players, all sub-six-footers on the verge of tears, listened to their coach give golden nuggets of abstract wisdom like: "We didn't play any defense. We had too many turnovers. We didn't rebound. You know what's wrong with y'all? You just don't want it. You gotta want it."
Good stuff coach. Thanks for the tips.

We can laugh and say this isn't us. But I know for a fact I've done this more than once. Most coaches are confident people with high expectations. And unmet expectations can lead to irrational anger. And irrational anger is a big disconnect with players.

So, we must be careful, no matter how realistic we think our expectations are, that we don't get angry with our players when they are doing their best. Sometimes, they're just over-matched. That doesn't mean they aren't Warriors. It means they have the opportunity to respond like Warriors. Learn and get better.

THE ULTIMATE VARIABLE—POISE

So, we got this all figured out—*Will* in competition is the determination and abilities one exerts to achieve a win. Easy game.
Lee Corso would say, "Not so fast, my friend."

Theory is always a good start, but it's so basic. Static. A hint at reality. Remember, we don't live in a vacuum where theory can solve all our problems. Because life is dynamic, it throws monkey wrenches into our plans. Exciting.

The reality of the will looks more like this:

decision + (Determination)(Ability) =
a higher probability of desired outcome (as long as we don't lose our poise)

I understand why this equation wouldn't market like the first one. People love certainty. It gives us the warm and fuzzies. Maybe because there is so much scarcity of certainty. But sorry, folks. There won't be any easy formulas with no moving parts here. We live in an unpredictable world. The real world.

The monkey wrench (variable) here is poise. A team can have the ability and determination to impose their will, but fail because they lose their poise. It happens all the time, and it only takes one person—player or coach—losing control of their emotions to wreck a great opportunity.

Lack of poise undermines the will to win. All the more reason we as coaches should work hard to set realistic expectations and become masters of poise.

Members of a Warrior Culture (coaches included) decide to be Warriors before the games begin.
It's easier to keep our poise in the heat of battle when we've already decided how we're going to act in the face of adversity.

PART 4:
Peace of Mind for Warriors

BUCS: GATTI/WARD

Anyone who followed boxing in the 2000s feels something in their souls when they hear Gatti/Ward. Many boxing analysts call their first fight the fight of the decade. Some call it the fight of the century. A few analysts go as far to say it was the greatest competitive event of all time.

They didn't fight for a belt. They fought because they loved a great fight, and in each other, the worthiest of opponents had been found. So they fought two more times.

Most people have heard of Mickey Ward because of the movie, *The Fighter*, starring Mark Wahlberg.[58] Many only know Arturo Gatti because of his tragic death and the mysterious circumstances of it. But boxing fans can't hear one name without pairing it with the other.

A working-class brawler from south Boston. And a skilled Italian-born scrapper prone to throw strategy out the window and lead with his face. It was the perfect matchup. As if Joe Louis and Rocky Marciano, grieved by the scandals and flashy promotions that produced years of boring fights that didn't live up to the hype, conspired from beyond the grave to put Gatti and Ward on a collision course. One that would bring the "fight" back into prize fighting.

---

[58] *The Fighter*. Directed by David O. Russell. Performances by Mark Wahlberg and Christian Bale. Paramount Pictures, 2010.

Midway through their first fight, the arena was electric, and fight fans were more than getting their money's worth. After round 9, the greatest 3 minutes of competition I've seen with my own eyes, everyone in the building knew they were witnessing first-hand an epic moment of boxing history.

Both men went down in that fight. Both men came up swinging. And both men showed that the heart of a Warrior transcends results, titles, and prizes. You could see it in their faces during the bout. As if, in their mind, they were like, "Finally, I've met my match."

Ward won the first fight by decision. In an interview, ring-side commentator Jim Lampley recalled running into distraught Gatti manager Pat Lynch in a hallway after the fight. Lampley told him, "No one who follows boxing will remember, even 6 months from now, who won this fight because both fighters have been elevated by the experience of what they did here."

Arturo Gatti bounced back and won the second fight, displaying his technically superior skill set. This would set up an epic rubber match, which Mickey Ward had said would be his last.

Gatti controlled the early rounds until he broke his right hand on a shot to Ward's hip in round 4, forcing him to fight the next few rounds throwing mostly his left. Ward took advantage, and the fight turned into a brawl, putting both men in the alley they loved the most.

The fight ended how everyone expected it to. In the last minute of their 30th round, the Warriors stood toe to toe and exchanged bombs in the center of the ring. Photographers captured snapshots of the action that contorted their faces, sending mists of sweat and blood through the air. Both men, exhausted, refused to go down. It was the way it had to end. When the bell rang, they embraced.

After their third fight, Ward made good on his word and retired. And the two fighters became friends, as Ward would put it, "Blood Brothers." Ward even trained him for the last fight of his career. And after Arturo Gatti's life was tragically cut short, Mickey Ward gave the eulogy at his funeral. Nobody knew Arturo Gatti better than Mickey Ward.

On a rainy October Monday in 2018, our first day of conditioning began with a locker room film session. I wanted them to see what Warriors looked like in action. To feel the emotions invoked when you witness impossible courage. To see what competitive respect looks like. To understand why the Warrior hunts for the great fight, and why he loves it.

During a real fight, Warriors become the physical incarnation of respect, showing the world what they love most about themselves—Their heart. They fully realize who they've always wanted to be. Who they were born to be.

We watched a fight that took place before our freshman were born. There aren't many teenage boxing historians, but I didn't care. That just meant I had some fresh material for them.

And this is who I am. I love boxing, even though I never so much as competed as an amateur. There is no competition where athletes compete as nakedly as boxing. Teddy Atlas calls the ring, "The chamber of truth" because character will shine and weakness will always be exposed during a good fight.

I wanted our guys to see what that looked like. I'm sure they thought we were about to watch clips that would teach them about basketball, or perhaps, preview our offensive philosophy. That would come later. Our priority was the Warrior Way.

They sat in their lockers with no idea that watching this fight could inspire the Warrior inside them. I framed it like this:

"This isn't a championship bout. Neither fighter is ranked in the top 50 fighters in history. But none of that matters. It's the best fight I've ever seen. And if you've ever wondered what being a Warrior looks like, here it is.[59] It's hard to watch these guys battle without wanting to be a better competitor.

"When you compete like this, respect comes with it. And if you want that kind of respect, then pay attention. These guys *fight*. Not for wins. Not for trophy or belt. Not so they can see their name in the paper. Warriors fight like this because they love the fighter in their soul. And they want to show the world.

---

[59] www.youtu.be/D5mRv3xGY80

"All a Warrior wants is a great fight against a worthy opponent. They crave it. That fight that pushes them to the physical and mental edge. To a place where they have to reach deep down and find something in them that keeps them on their feet, throwing bombs.

"And a Warrior wants to be that worthy opponent to someone else. When they find a fight like this, nothing else matters except the fight itself. They get lost in it. Like an out-of-body experience. Nerves—gone. Stress—gone. Posing—gone. All that's left is pure competition and pure hearts. I give you Arturo Gatti and Mickey Ward. Men, this is a crash course in Warrior Culture."

We watched the entire fight. Our guys didn't know going in who won or lost. With each passing round, our locker room got louder. They yelled at the screen. One stood and closed a fist over his mouth after a rib shattering body shot that sent Gatti to his knees in that legendary 9th round. Then Jaws dropped when Gatti recovered and took the fight right back to Ward.

Watching the tense last seconds of the final tenth round with my team, it felt like watching it for the first time. It's hard to watch that fight without being challenged to be a tougher person. Ward won by decision, but our guys understood *why* the result wasn't all that mattered. They loved Ward. They loved Gatti. They loved that fight. The result was an asterisk next to greatness.

After the fight, our team went upstairs to play pickup. Intense competition was our conditioning routine. And they absolutely got after it. Each defender picked up their man full court. If you wanted to advance the ball, you had to earn every floorboard.

Our coaches didn't instruct. We just watched them throw themselves into the battle.[60] The competitive atmosphere was palpable, and our guys played themselves into great shape.

That first week, every day before pickup, we watched a great round of boxing. On Tuesday, we watched round 10 of Holyfield/Bowe 1.
Wednesday, round 1 of Hagler/Hearns.
Thursday, round 15 of Norton/Holmes.
Friday, round 10 of Corrales/Castillo.
And on Saturday, we finished the week with round 9 of Gatti/Ward 1, coming full circle.

They witnessed the best in the best. The courage, the competitiveness, the mental challenge, and heart. Sure, I'm waxing a little poetic here, romanticizing something that some people don't believe matters in the grand scheme of things. But sports matter so much to so many because it's not just the sport that matters. It's what it can do to elevate the mind, body, and soul of a human being. In my experience, it's

---

[60] It must be noted, that these pickup games did get salty at times. So much so that we, as coaches, had to step in and let the guys know that toughness isn't throwing a punch, being a bully, or losing your cool during a basketball game. That is fake toughness. Real toughness is competing and never, EVER, never backing down to anyone for even a second. Real toughness is getting worked and still battling to figure it out. If we watch boxing with our team, we had better articulate fake toughness vs. real toughness before we compete or we may end up with a team of punch throwers and cheap shotters that end up in the newspaper for all the wrong reasons. We watch the fights with a metaphorical eye, learning from their courage and competitive drive. It's intentional mental practice for the mentally tough players our guys want to become.

spiritual. **Sports isn't life and death, but it's one of the best practices for real life we can get.**

High school education is enhanced by competitive sports. I've always felt that the most important things I have learned in my entire education were things of the soul. Of the mind. And many of these things, I learned through sports.

Being beaten by worthy opponents and picking myself up to find a way. The work ethic and critical thinking any level of mastery requires. The growth mindset to become someone who stands out amongst a crowd of capable people. How to respond when my plans get turned upside down. How to be a great teammate and enhance the performance of others. How to listen and communicate.

When we see a vision of someone we want to become, something clicks. That's inspiration. A coach can give their players that vision, inspire them to own it, hold them accountable when they fall short, and most importantly, notice when they answer the bell and take a step in the right direction.

The science of sport (X's and O's) is necessary in coaching, but it's arbitrary when compared to the science of impact. Nobody will care about the high school state championship somebody won 30 years ago. But if a player who had a role on that championship team, lives a life aligned with the Warrior Way, the impact he/she can have on this world could be astounding.

At the very least, the Warrior will have lived a life that will be remembered. They will have been respected. Loved. Grown men like legendary HBO boxing commentator Jim Lampley are moved to tears when they talk about Gatti and Ward.

Scores, hundreds, thousands, maybe even hundreds of thousands of people may be inspired to live a better life because a young kid unleashed the Warrior within after watching Arturo Gatti and Mickey Ward fight.

The fiery chain reaction of inspiration that one person can ignite by showing one hour of courage can affect generations.

Chapter 8

Mindfulness and Optimism

Statistically, today's teenagers are more depressed than they've ever been.[61] And it makes sense when you take into account the pressures that social media puts on them daily. I grew up in the 90s and didn't have to deal with Snap culture and the magnified need for social acceptance that comes with it. It's hard for them.

25 years ago, coaches may have been able to focus primarily on the physical and strategic. But when it comes to the challenges our kids face today and the affects these challenges have on their psyches, we don't have the luxury of ignoring the mind and soul anymore.

And even if we could, why would we want to? We know that teenage depression and anxiety is a problem on the rise. And who better to help in this area than their mentors? The champions of their Warrior Culture. Their coaches.

---

[61]   https://health.usnews.com/wellness/for-parents/articles/2019-04-22/teen-depression-is-on-the-rise

Maybe we're unfamiliar with the practice of mindfulness ourselves. Well, we talk to our players about getting out of their comfort zones, and this might be a perfect opportunity to live what we preach. There is a need. And as the leader of our Warrior Culture, we should embrace a complete training model to maximize the staying power of the life skills we teach.

Forcing life to come to a stop, even if it's only for 10 minutes, can do wonders for our peace of mind. We know this is true, but why don't we let teens in on this secret habit that enhances our lives? Maybe we don't know how to teach it. That's fine and completely understandable. If that's the case, this practice is worth outsourcing to an expert.

Phil Jackson knew the Warrior trains the physical, the mental, *and* the spiritual. And he showed his players how to do it. Miyamoto Musashi knew it, too, and wrote about it often. Those guys seem to have a handle on the Warrior Way.

Yoga and mindfulness sessions for our student-athletes will add value to their preparation for performance. But more importantly, it sets a time to work on the mental and the spiritual. Again, we don't have to run these sessions ourselves. We can find someone familiar with mindfulness practices and Yoga. They aren't hard to find. Maybe it's one of our athletic trainers. Maybe it's a mindfulness coach or sports psychologist in our area. Maybe it's a Yoga teacher at our school.

Recently, I became a Yoga teacher. My goal for our high school Yoga class wasn't complicated. I wanted the class to reduce stress. I'd done Yoga, but never as a consistent practice. Three weeks into the semester, our daily Yoga routine was a valuable enhancement to my life.

I never did Yoga as a player. I knew Phil Jackson was big into mindfulness and Zen, but I never understood his *why*. Honestly, to me, it seemed like soft, hippie, woo-woo stuff. Not for a guy like me.

I've never been more wrong in my life. We began doing Yoga sessions with our high school team. I had to sell them on it at first, but one sentence makes that fairly easy, "If it worked for Phil, MJ, and Kobe, maybe we should have an open mind."

The physical, mental, and spiritual benefits of Yoga are well documented. The best thing about Yoga is we can customize sequences and routines to fit the needs of our team. Our focus was on flexibility and clarity of mind. The all-encompassing, yet abstract word for this clarity is mindfulness. It's awareness. But awareness of what? And why? To what end?

For a sports guy like me to understand a mental practice as grandiose as mindfulness, it had to be broken down to small parts. This is what we do in sports. We train the micro to prepare for the macro.

So, we're gonna hit this quick because I'm sure you aren't reading this to learn about Yoga. But if mindfulness has always been important to the Warrior, we can't leave it out.

BREATHING

Our breath is powerful, and we rarely notice it. When we give it our attention, it calms the mind. Deep breathing techniques affect the brain by giving it more oxygen. This provides a better chance for clarity of thought, something high school kids and adults alike can't have too much of.

SELF-AWARENESS

It's often challenging for anyone to be self-aware, much less a high school student still figuring out who he/she is. But self-awareness is a valuable trait for human beings.

Self-aware people have more emotional intelligence. They more likely to improve themselves. And more likely to recognize and stop self-destructive habits. They are also more honest, humble, secure, and empathetic.

Meditation has almost become a necessity for many people. We may need to be intentional about slowing down. Our thoughts need our recognition. They need acceptance, or rejection, or at the least, measurement for rationality.

VISUALIZATION

Visualizing performance with a quiet mind is a powerful, proactive mental practice for impending high-pressure moments. Many coaches spend most of their time on the physical—skill development, execution, conditioning, etc. But Phil Jackson was way ahead of his time in his approach to preparing the mind. He dedicated blocks of time for it, and the primary beneficiaries of his emphasis on the mental game were his players.

From Damian Lillard to Kerri Walsh and Misty May-Treanor, most of today's professional athletes have strict pregame visualization routines.[62] It might be time for amateurs to take note of this elite habit of successful people.

TEAM YOGA AND VISUALIZATION IN PRACTICE

In a world that screams, "GO, GO, GO," today's teenagers rarely slow down and get quiet with their thoughts long enough to get clarity through

---

[62] In an article by Anna Williams on mindbodygreen.com, World-class skier Lindsay Vonn said, "I always visualize the run before I do it. By the time I get to the start gate, I've run that race 100 times in my head, picturing how I'll take the turns." It's not just athletes that employ the power of visualization. Actors Jim Carrey and Will Smith claim visualization has played a key role of their success. (www.mindbodygreen.com/amp/articles/8-successful-people-who-use-the-power-of-visualization--20630)

contemplation. And I can see why they don't. They have so many interesting, and often addictive, things competing for their attention. And winning.

Most of them probably don't know how to slow down. And I'm sure many don't even realize how much mindfulness could help their peace of mind. We can help them by showing them a practice that could help them.

Here's an example of the sessions we do with our players: 15-minute max. Deep stretch with a Yoga sequence. Our players like the Warrior Flow.[63] At the conclusion of the sequence, we instruct them to close their eyes, sit up straight, and breathe. Four second inhales. Four second exhales.

After a minute or two of breathing, It's story time, baby. This is where the magic happens. We often tell personal anecdotes or a Warrior story from history that might inspire them to play with courage. The background music always fits the mood. On the road, we have players who would rather us forget our clipboards than the Bluetooth speaker.

In our visualization exercises, we encourage them to close their eyes and see their performance as if they were watching themselves in a movie. We narrate (using names) sequences that our players will perform in the game. They picture themselves making extra passes, grabbing rebounds, taking charges, and knocking down shots. In the end, we give them a few

---

[63] We enjoy irony.

minutes with their visualization and reflections while the music rolls.

OPTIMISM FOR STRUGGLING HIGH SCHOOL TEAMS

John Heywood is famous for his quote, "Rome wasn't built in a day..."
But many don't know that there is a second part of that quote,
"...but they were laying bricks every hour."

In building a program, every brick is necessary for a lasting foundation. It's the constant work that gets the job done. Sometimes, the challenge lies in helping our players see the big picture during hard times. Optimism plays an important role when our teams or players are struggling.

When hard work, dedication, and a growth mindset are present in our culture, there is always possibility that the future will look better than the present. Relentless optimism can help our players. Optimism implies belief. It's a demonstration of hope that develops immunity to the emotional roller coaster of a season contingent on wins and losses. It puts intense focus on the process and celebrates it.

We can coach kids hard and be optimistic. We can even raise our voice and be intense. They just need to know that we *know* they're capable of more. And that we *believe* they'll get there. When our coaching is about belief, even our criticisms become honoring to our athletes. That's relentless optimism.

The way this works in practice is taking the time to recognize our wins big and small, acknowledging team improvements and personal breakthroughs. When our teams are inexperienced or not talented enough, we may have to find wins to celebrate. That may look like winning second halves, or quarters, or even halves of quarters.

If we're down 20, "Let's cut this thing to 15 in the first 4 minutes of the 2nd half, and then we'll reassess." If we hit that goal, it's a mission accomplished. And we should be excited about it and then move forward. It's another thing that's easy to say and hard to do, but getting excited about a "win" when we've been getting beaten down reminds our kids that we aren't going to give up on them. Especially if we're coaching young kids, those moments will pay off down the road.

As our teams get older and better, we'll be fighting the opposite battle. We'll become the team showing up as a heavy favorite. The players will be so competitive that they'll be disappointed if they don't play to their potential. And at times, they'll get complacent with a shade of arrogance. That's normal, but if it happens, we'll have to find ways to challenge them. To bring them back to earth. To make things tougher. And maybe even, manufacture a "loss" or two.

Yes, we want to teach our kids to be Warriors. We want relentlessness that refuses to quit and desires peak performance. But when losing a lot, it's a balancing act. Celebrating and acknowledging growth motivates people to chase more growth. And if we've gone weeks without having much fun (Read: Losing), we should militant about nurturing the fun of the game while we're getting better. Nobody can suck the fun out of a sport like coaches who take themselves too seriously. We've had to learn that the hard way.

Navigating our tone is constantly reading the room and giving our team what they need. We're teaching them life-time habits and mental approaches that must produce growth regardless of the situation.

Chapter 9

Glorious End

"He who fears loss has been beaten already."
— Kano Jigoro (Creator of Judo)

Homer's epic poem, *The Illiad,* follows one of the greatest Warriors in mythology, the demi-god Achilles as he slaughters his way to the gates of Troy on behalf of the Greeks. In literature, he was a bad man, one of the most prolific killers to ever step foot on a battlefield.

But maybe the most interesting character in *The Illiad* was the leader of the Trojan army, Hector. He's more relatable because he was a mere mortal just like us and had something to lose every time he strapped on his armor. In real life, there is no glorious victory without risk.

Hector killed the brother of Achilles in battle. And when Achilles found out, he was more than pissed. He rode straight to the Trojan castle walls to call out Hector for a fight. It was a sight nobody inside the

Trojan walls wanted to see. Achilles was said to be blessed by the gods, even part god himself. I imagine, no matter how great the Warrior, it would have felt like walking out to play high stakes one on one vs. LeBron James. Or a being challenged to a sprint for your life against Usain Bolt.

Hector's wife, holding their newborn baby, stood by his side and begged him to stay where he might be safe. She tried her best to reason with him, "Dearest, your own great strength will be your death, and you have no pity on your little son, nor on me, ill-starred, who soon must be your widow."

She knew the long odds. Achilles was that dangerous. And Hector had so much to lose, but suppose for a moment that he relented to his wife and stayed within the walls. Could he have been the Warrior if he ducked his chance in one of the biggest moments of the Trojan war? Could he have still been the legendary Hector, breaker of horses, leader of the Trojan army, slaughterer of the Greeks?

But he knew the men under his command would succumb to their own fears if he backed down from this fight. How could he expect them to lay their life on the line for Troy if he, the champion of Trojan Warrior Culture, wasn't willing to do it himself?

As he processed his options, he responded in true Warrior fashion, "All these things are in my mind also, lady; yet I would feel deep shame before the Trojans... if like a coward I were to shrink aside from the fighting."

And he went out to face the end of his days, inspiring his men to face their biggest fears and fight anyway. And he rightfully took his place as a legend of Trojan Warrior Culture.

HOLYFIELD/BOWE 1

When I was a kid. I had a poster in my room of Evander Holyfield. Chiseled with an angry brow and two title belts around each shoulder, and one around his waist. "The Warrior."

In round ten of Holyfield's first fight with Riddick Bowe, Bowe hit him with one of the nastiest uppercuts I've ever seen. Holyfield's eyes glazed over, blood and drool fell from his mouth, and he stumbled into the ropes. He should've gone down. But somehow, he stayed on his feet.

Bowe smelled blood in the water and went for the KO with a vicious barrage on Holyfield, who was only being held up by the ropes. Holyfield desperately used both arms to block his head. He looked done.

I was 12 and scared. Holyfield was my hero. Apollo Creed seizing on the canvas in *Rocky 4* flashed in my mind. And for the first time in my life, I wanted Holyfield to lose. I wanted him to go down. I didn't wanna watch "The Real Deal" get killed in the ring.

Jelly-legged, Holyfield finally escaped as Bowe caught his breath for a few seconds, having punched himself out. They clinched, and Holyfield came out of it throwing wildly, so hard he almost fell. Both men, exhausted, clinched a few more times. And at the 1:10 mark, Holyfield, with his right eye swollen shut, hit Bowe with an uppercut of his own followed by a flurry of big shots.

The crowd went wild, adrenaline rushed, and Holyfield came alive, dancing in the ring and landing jabs, hooks, and overhand rights.

To this day, I can still hear the voices of the ring-side commentators,[64]
"Look at Holyfield. What a Warrior!"
"He's got a heart."
"If he weighs 205, his heart weighs about 204."

Bowe fought back. They fought well after the bell rang to end the round. It wasn't dirty fighting. They just lost themselves in the battle and probably couldn't hear the bell because of the raucous crowd.

When the referee finally broke them up, they headed to their respective corners. If you watch closely, Bowe looked at Holyfield as he passed and tapped him twice on the belly with his glove. A subtle gesture of respect. Like, "Wow, man. You *are* 'The Real Deal'." That was the night Evander Holyfield became "The Warrior."

---

[64] That may or may not be because I've watched this round dozens of times on YouTube. www.youtu.be/6GngvYoQj4

Bucs

"Generally speaking, the Way of the Warrior is resolute acceptance of death."

—Miyamoto Musashi

For even the most talented, pure-hearted seniors in high school, the uncertain future can be a terrifying proposition. If members of a team love each other, it can make the thought of the season being over more paralyzing. The inevitable end brings fear. Not just the end itself, but more specifically, the part the individual might play in the collective heartbreak. Failure often means letting down friends and family and missing an opportunity for an experience they'd never forget.

Let's be honest, that's a lot to lose for teenagers. Pretending that it's not is forgetting what it was like to be a teenager. And often, it's forgetting what it's like to be human.

Even as adults, fear can make us hesitant in our decision making. We might play it safe. Not jumping at big opportunities even though the risk is manageable. And as a result, we might stay the same. We'd survive but wouldn't survive *and* advance. In competitive ventures, we often have to risk something we've gained to advance. Otherwise, we don't make it to the big stage.

Nobody becomes a pro at anything without accepting the real possibility of falling flat on their face. Pros know this, so they shoot. A lot. And they miss. A lot. And when they miss, at least they can sleep at night because they had the courage to take the shot.

Sure, they might lose sleep for a night or two, due to being a pissed off competitor, but they get over it because there are more shots to take. It's not missing shots that tortures people for years. It's not taking them. Or becoming gun-shy to the point they only shoot if it's a sure thing. That's making a career out of being Nameless. Some people can live with that, not Warriors.

Fear of loss makes players hesitant. And hesitant players lose. Even their aura becomes a walking defeat because they spend so many hours in that fear, always looking over their shoulder, worried about the next loss.

If we are to become Warriors, our battles will come with fear, and our victories will come with risk. Young athletes *need* to know this. They need to know that Warriors name their fear so they can overcome it and calculate risk so they can manage it to their advantage.

In tournament sports, teams are forced to risk it all. And most, like Hector, will lose in the end. This is terrifying for the kids who care the most. **But for our players to conquer their fears, they have to recognize and feel their emotions without being handicapped by them.** Coaches can help if we guide them to this recognition and feel their emotions with them. It's an empathetic task, understanding and validating without patronizing. **In confronting our insecurities and fears, we take away their power over us.**

Those who love the battle (and who love life) lose themselves in the experience and make the most out of what they have. And the most out of every moment. And sometimes, they even achieve the feat of the great Warrior—Their name outlives their life.

The 2018-2019 Bucs faced the end of their season on the road in the region tournament against a talented team with two Division 1 signees. This tough draw was a result of freezing up in the District tournament against a cross-town rival we'd swept in the regular season. We got the big eyes. They whipped us. We had to go through the experience. And we owned it, vowing to never succumb to the fear again.

We competed hard in our region tournament underdog game, but were outmatched and outsized and found ourselves down by 20 with 6 minutes to play. I called a timeout.

"Well fellas, if this is where it has to happen, this is where it has to happen. You get to show who you really are. Go down fighting. This is your chance to inspire and earn respect. Your Warrior's death. Leave your soul out there and amaze everyone in this gym with your effort. We've wanted this all year. It's your Spartan moment. Make it epic. Make yourselves proud."

And they did. After four minutes of flying all over the floor, boxing out, taking charges, scraping, and scrapping, we'd thrown a Molotov cocktail on a game that seemed over minutes before. With two minutes to play, we were down six, and our opponents called their second timeout of that stretch.

We had all the momentum. Our electrified bench raced on the floor to celebrate the will of their Warrior teammates with chest bumps and high fives. Against all odds, a win was in our sights. We could taste it.

But there's no fairy tale ending here, either. After a few missed shots, a few bad breaks, two starters fouling out, and clutch free throws by our opponent, we were down 12 with 30 seconds left. I emptied our bench.

But our men were Warriors, fighting with honor to the bitter end. That team achieved their glorious end and became the benchmark for our program moving forward. They were proud of themselves. And so was everyone wearing Buccaneer blue that night.

The next year, with five Warrior seniors, we won our first District Championship since making the jump to the private school division of our state association. A few weeks later, they earned their glorious end in the State Tournament quarterfinals against a better team. It was an epic fight on a neutral court, and our only sadness was that it was our last fight together. I'll never forget that post-game locker room experience. Nobody grieves things they don't have great passion for. We'd earned our pain. And it felt good.

This group of young men had lived through tough times personally and athletically. They had been knocked down, but they got up, got better, embraced Warrior Culture, said "GOOD", inspired their entire school, and now had a Championship banner to show for it.

There's no better feeling than giving our players something they can take with them after the ball stops bouncing. It's surreal to know that, whatever difficulties life throws at them, they can always come back to their home gym and see that banner and remember their Warrior Culture...

We were the most resilient, most respectable, most worthy opponent. When people watched us play, they left saying, "Man, those kids are tough."

Back in those rowdy gyms, no matter what went wrong or what the score, I was a Warrior. And when I look in the mirror tonight, I'll smile and remember, I'm still that. Just more practiced. Better.

Life's not supposed to be easy. I never expected it to be. But I know who I am. And however bad I feel right now, I know I'm ready for this. I'm not going down. But even if I do, I won't stay down. And I'm getting up swinging. Some dogs you can't break. I'm that dog. Adversity's worthiest opponent.

I remember who I decided to be a long time ago. And I'll stay on this Warrior Path until the end of my days.

They will remember my name. **Warrior.**

ACKNOWLEDGMENTS

In 2013, Cole Rose, the head coach at Boyd Buchanan, told me his team, led by 7 rising seniors, froze in the big game the year before. He told me they were missing something. That's how this conversation started. The Warrior Way had lived in our hearts, but we'd never given it words until we tackled this problem together.

So, Cole... Good talks, man. Thanks for helping make the Warrior Way tangible for our players. You gave an idea words, then gave it to your team, and they won that big game.

And Dustin Walker, PV, Nick Huge, and Charlie McHarney, who dropped so much wisdom on me while I worked on this book. Thank you. You guys are the real deal.

About the Author

Josh Templeton is a former college assistant basketball coach and current high school coach. He is the author of the coach's kid memoir; *I Played for my Dad for 9 Years, and We Still Talk.* Available on Amazon Kindle.

If you enjoyed *Warrior Culture: The Warrior Way for High School Teams,* please leave a review on Amazon and share it on social media.

And hit me up on Twitter. I love to connect with other coaches and hear what works for your teams.
Twitter:
@joshtempleton37

Made in the USA
Columbia, SC
29 January 2021